An Essay on the Statement "Humanity before Religion"

An Essay on the Statement "Humanity before Religion": Foundations and Analysis

Ḥāmid ibn ʿUmar ibn Ḥafīẓ

TABAH RESEARCH

TABAH ESSAYS SERIES | NUMBER 7 | 2021
ISSN: 2077-4850

An Essay on the Statement "Humanity before Religion": Foundations
and Analysis
ISBN: 978-9948-8607-2-3

Summary

In this essay the author carefully provides the reader with an analysis of the theological claim 'Humanity before Religiosity' which was the subject of a series of talks and articles written by Habib Ali al-Jifri between 2012 and 2014 that led to vivid debates concerning the validity and benefit of such statement. The author commences with a concise summary of the main arguments of the statement 'Humanity before Religiosity' and proceeds with a careful analysis of the main critiques against the statement. Hamid aims to illustrate not only the invalidity of these arguments but also to reiterate the necessity of 'Humanity before Religiosity' through a careful cursory reading of pivotal texts in the Islamic tradition.

About the Author

ḤĀMID IBN ʿUMAR IBN ḤAFĪẒ (1997) is an independent researcher with a focus on theology, and contemporary social and ethical issues. As a native of Hadramawt (Yemen) he started his studies under the tutelage of his father Ḥabīb ʿUmar ibn Ḥafīẓ and went on to graduate from Dar al-Mustafa, an Islamic educational Seminary in Tarim. At Dar al-Mustafa he studied the various Islamic sciences including: Qur'an, Exegesis, Prophetic traditions (Hadith), Jurisprudence (Ūsūl al-fiqh) and Sacred Law (fiqh) as well as Creed (ʿaqīdah) and principles of Islamic spirituality (Taṣṣawuf). He has also studied privately with prominent scholars from Egypt and Syria to further deepen his knowledge and expertise.

In the Name of Allah, the Most Merciful
and Compassionate

Praise be to God, the Lord of all the worlds; and may His blessings and peace be upon our master Muhammad, his kinfolk, and his Companions.

One of our beloved teachers has expressed the vital importance of the health of one's natural human disposition (*fiṭrah*). Since the receptivity towards religion is dependent upon the purity and clarity of one's *fiṭrah*, which functions as a mirror for the lights of obedience to be intensified, he expressed this sentiment with the statement "Humanity before religion."[1] Subsequently, the statement stirred up some confusion and was subject to quite some controversy. The purpose of this modest essay is to briefly explicate the real intent behind this statement and the validity and evidence for it from within the Islamic tradition.

DISSECTING THE TERMS

PRELIMINARY REMARKS

Judgement is a branch of conception, and acceptance and rejection can neither stand for due consideration nor for acceptance

---

1. Translator's note: "Religion" here is used in the sense of religious observance.

except on the firm grounds of understanding and comprehension with regards to the thing that is to be judged. It is a general principle utilized and propagated within the Islamic tradition, such as by Imam Abū Ḥāmid al-Ghazālī (d. 505/1111) – may God grant him His Mercy – who states that "the acceptance or rejection of a position must be subsequent to its intelligibility".[2] I found that most of the criticisms directed at the statement "Humanity before religion" are based on distorted conceptions projected onto it by those critics, while the intended meaning is nowhere near what they have understood. One ought to give due consideration to the possible meanings of this statement, and then to examine those possibilities against the set of acceptable meanings within the framework of the Islamic theological and legal tradition. Only then can one confirm or deny them properly. It goes without saying that the default stance with respect to the speech of rational agents is that it be protected against trivialization; that is, if the speaker has not specified the precise meaning which may be semantically supported by the statement, then one should not automatically reduce its meaning to exclude this particular meaning. Thus it is even more obvious in this case, wherein the said speaker has clarified what they meant on numerous occasions.

So in order to follow the aforementioned methodology, we must first engage in an exposition of exactly what we mean when we talk about the concept of religion and the concept of humanity.

HUMANITY (AL-INSĀNIYYAH)

Lexically, the term "humanity" denotes nobility (*murū'ah*) in the Arabic language and that is why nobility is likewise defined in its terms, per *Lisān al-ʿArab* and *Tāj al-ʿArūs*.[3]

---

2.   al-Ghazālī, *al-Iqtiṣād*, 223.

3   Ibn Manẓūr, *Lisān al-ʿArab*, 1:154; al-Zabīdī, *Tāj al-ʿArūs*, s.v. "M-R-ʾ", 1:427.

There are also several definitions for nobility; one of the most comprehensive is presented by al-Fayyūmī (d. 770/1368) – may God grant him His Mercy – in *al-Miṣbāḥ al-Munīr*, stating: "[It is a set of] personal virtues whose due consideration make man privy to the highest moral character and the most beautiful habits," which was cited verbatim by al-Zabīdī in *Tāj al-ʿArūs*.[4]

Just as humanity denotes a certain form of being which drives one to achieve noble character in general, it is also used to denote some of those virtues in particular. That is why it is often explicated in their terms, as when al-Aḥnaf ibn Qays (d. 72/691) – may God grant him His Mercy – was asked "What is humanity?" and he answered: "Humility in authority, forgiveness in power, and giving [alms] without condescension."[5]

Whether one uses the term humanity to denote the form which drives one to virtue in general or to some virtues in particular, the basic intention is to refer to this quality and habit that is established in the self and not merely the actions, similar to the case of virtue, even though the term is often used to denote actions.[6]

Al-Rāghib al-Iṣfahānī (d. 502/1108) – may God grant him His Mercy – defined humanity in his *al-Dharīʿah* as "the individual virtues specific to mankind". This definition is more comprehensive than the previous definitions insofar as it includes every virtue unique to humanity, whether it manifests in an ethos or a habit or does not manifest at all, such as the health of one's nature, the sensitivity of one's faculties, and

---

4.   al-Fayyūmī, *al-Miṣbāḥ al-Munīr*, s.v. "M-R-ʾ", 356; al-Zabīdī, *Tāj al-ʿArūs*, s.v. "M-R-ʾ", 1:427.

5.   al-Samarqandī, *Tanbīh al-Ghāfilīn*, 210.

6.   See, for example, al-Ghazālī, *Iḥyāʾ ʿUlūm al-Dīn*, 5:189–91. From this exposition, one knows the falsity of the objection of one author based on the idea that "humanity" is strictly to *act* in ethical ways, for he begins his discussion by stating "If humanity meant to act ethically …".

other similar features which are unique to humanity and are neither ethics nor habits.

In its contemporary Arabic usage, the meaning of humanity remained the same. In *al-Muʿjam al-Wasīṭ*, a twentieth-century lexicon, the following definition is presented: "Humanity: the opposite of savagery (*bahīmiyyah*), and the set of general attributes unique to humankind, or the set of all individuals of the human species of which these attributes are true."[7]

The definite article "al-" in the word "*al-insāniyyah*" is known in Arabic linguistics as the definite article of identity or of figurative reality. As the definite article of identity, it is that which "signifies the reality of a thing insofar as it is realized in its individual instances in an indefinite way",[8] and therefore the term humanity applies to all the virtues that pertain to the human being.

It remains to be noted that knowledge regarding whether a virtue is implied by the notion of humanity may be reached independently by reason. Take, for example, the fact that, through the faculty of reason, we conclude that lying is reprehensible, a vice which is contrary to the entailments of reason.[9] In a similar fashion, one may extend this to other virtues which fall under the concept of humanity and this is why the notion of humanity is so widespread among human beings, irrespective of their religious practice. It is on this basis that it is valid to attribute human virtues to reason by stating that they are virtues of the mind insofar as it is possible for reason to grasp their goodness and virtue.

---

7. al-Majmaʿ al-Lughah al-ʿArabiyyah, *al-Muʿjam al-Wasīṭ*, 1:50.
8. al-Dasūqī, *Ḥāshiyat al-Dasūqī*, 96.
9. For a similar line of reasoning, see al-ʿAynī, *ʿUmdat al-Qārī*, 1:85.

The gist of the relation between humanity and the primordial disposition (*fiṭrah*) is that the latter is "the set of attributes which every being has at the origin of its creation",[10] or, put differently, it is "that original form in which man is made"[11] and "the original form prepared to receive normativity (*al-dīn*)".[12] The primordial disposition (*fiṭrah*) has other definitions similar to these, and from a general overview of these definitions it becomes clear that it is not identical to humanity, namely, those "virtues which are specific to man"; rather, it is the state of man which prepares him to acquire those virtues and it is hardly possible for one to be separated from the other. Therefore, the well-being of one's primordial disposition entails the obtaining of humanity.

The connection between the primordial disposition and the higher virtues is brilliantly highlighted in al-Kafawī's (d. 1094/1683) definition of vice (*ʿayb*), which he states is "that which is not comprised by the primordial disposition", indicating that the primordial disposition is never void of virtues; indeed, they exist with it and are concomitant to it.

HUMANITY AND INTELLECT (ʿAQL)
Previously, we discussed that when virtues are attributed to the intellect, what is meant are those virtues which one comes to know by means of the intellect, which is humanity itself. The following ubiquitous statement testifies to this connection: "It is only called the *ʿaql* [intellect] because it constraints its subject from committing heinous acts, and that is why it is said, 'the vicious man is devoid of intellect.'"[13]

---

10.   al-Kafawī, *al-Kulliyyāt*, 587.
11.   al-Munāwī, *al-Tawqīf*, 348.
12.   al-Jurjānī, *al-Taʿrīfāt*, 168; see also al-Munāwī, *al-Tawqīf*, 348, citing Ibn Kamāl Pasha.
13. al-Bājūrī, Ḥāshiyat al-Bājūrī ... ʿalā Matn Abī Shujāʿ, 1:314; see also al-Ṣiddiqī,

Intellect may also denote the "praiseworthy composition of man in his actions and sayings",[14] in which case it refers to the fruit of humanity, for the praiseworthy composition of man in his actions and sayings is circumscribed by noble virtues and beautiful habits, which we saw previously are what humanity has a unique capacity for.

HUMANITY BEFORE RELIGION: THE TYPE OF PRIORITY INTENDED BY THE TERM BEFORE

That humanity is "before" religion indicates that it is prior to it; but priority is of several types and takes on different forms with respect to various expressions and aspects of analysis. Thus priority can be (1) in time, such as the priority of the existence of the father over his son; or (2) it can be in place, such as the priority of the one who leads the prayer over the followers behind him; or (3) it may be by cause, such as the priority of the motion of the finger to the motion of the ring on that particular finger. The motion of the finger is prior to the motion of the ring in the ontological sense due to its being the cause of the ring's motion, even though the motion of the finger and the ring occur at the same time in the external world. Lastly, (4) the priority of the term "before" can also mean a priority by nature, such as the priority of one over two.[15]

Now, since not all senses of priority are intended by this phrase (i.e. "Humanity before religion"), as is plainly clear, then which of these is best suited to this statement?

Both a priority by nature and a priority in time could reasonably be considered for this statement. The latter would mean that the existence of man is prior in time to the existence of

____

Dalīl al-Fāliḥīn, 2:237.
14. al-Kafawī, *al-Kulliyyāt*, 520.
15. See al-Ṣabbān, *Ḥāshiyat al-Ṣabbān*, 91.

religion, but the intention in the said phrase seems more aligned with the consideration of a priority by nature.[16]

The intended sense of priority in the term "before" is priority by nature, which has been calibrated as follows: "it is for the anterior [word] to be such that the posterior is dependent on it but without suggesting the anterior to be an efficient cause for it. This is the case of the number one in relation to two,

---

16. With this explication, the falsehood of one objection becomes evident, namely, the statement of some that "the first obligation on man is to have knowledge of his Creator and what follows from that in obligatory beliefs, then knowledge of what is obligatory for them in terms of actions …" to the end of this strange tirade. The person who states this has imagined that the priority intended in the statement is temporal priority, then they affirmed that temporal priority in terms of normative obligation! Then they objected by stating that the first obligation is knowledge! Such an objector has volunteered their own creativity in inventing means of the phrase which conform to the objections they have decided to direct against it.

It is also prescient to state here that there is no temporal priority among the obligations that pertain to the agent, such that one is obligatory first to the exclusion of the rest, and that the agent is not obligated by the rest of them, then the second obligation is directed to them, and so on. This is only the case according to those who believe that the obligation to know obtains by means of reason before the arrival of revelation, but according to the Ash'arī school, this is false. Rather, all obligations obtain for the agent at once by the mere fulfillment of the conditions of moral obligation and the receiving of sufficient knowledge of the Prophet Muhammad's call and mission. The discussions among Ash'arī scholars on the first obligation is only about what one must perform first, for it is not possible to worship God before having knowledge of God, even if the obligation to worship obtains for the agent simultaneously with the obligation to have knowledge of God. In other words, it is with regard to the priority among the *knowledge* of those obligations that pertain to him. That is, knowledge of the obligations obtains for the agent one after another, such that he first comes to know that knowledge of God is obligatory, then after believing in Him, he comes to know the rest of the obligations required of him. This ordering is not necessary either, for it could be the case that the agent first comes to know the mission of the Prophet by means of its signs, and through that, comes to know the existence of God and acquires knowledge. Nevertheless, the first ordering is the natural course of things, and that is why the Ash'arī scholars affirmed it, so that the law conforms to nature.

In summary, there is no temporal priority among moral obligations insofar as they relate to the agent, even though there is a temporal priority in carrying out those obligations, as the agent comes to have knowledge of those obliga-tions. For more, see al-Ghursī, *Badr al-Tamām*, 66–67.

and likewise the relation between conception and assent."[17] Therefore, the sense in which humanity is prior to religion is that the anterior meaning, namely humanity, relates to the posterior in that the posterior, namely religion, stands in need of it, without affirming that humanity is a *cause* of religion. *The importance of this qualification cannot be overstated.* When we discuss the meaning of the term "religion" in the statement that is subject to our analysis, we will expand on a few more aspects of this kind of priority.

In any case, the intention of the statement is not priority in nobility and importance as imagined by some, for they interpreted the statement as indicating a demotion of religion and the promotion of humanity, which is sometimes claimed by non-Muslims. However, the phrase is far from such interpretations; rather, as we have already seen, it is about natural priority in the sense that an instrument is prior to the purpose of the instrument, and a circumstance (*zarf*) is prior to the conditions it implies or brings about. So one's purposes and aims are nobler than that which achieves them, and this will be explicated further below.

RELIGION OR RELIGIOUS PRACTICE (AL-TADAYYUN)
The term "*al-tadayyun*" is derived from *al-dīn*, namely, what God has prescribed for humanity, and the form *al-tafaʿʿul* is to indicate emphasis and struggle, namely, "struggle and practice towards the fulfillment of an action".[18] Thus the meaning of religion (i.e. in the sense of observance) is the practice of the Islamic religion and struggling to apply its norms. It is also possible to express the meaning of religious observance as follows: the observance of God's religion by mankind, in their beliefs, their understanding of its contents, and in their prac-

---

17.   al-Bājūrī, *Ḥāshiyat al-Bājūrī ʿalā al-Sullam al-Munawraq*, 87.
18.   al-Jāwī al-Makkī, *Tadrīj al-Adānī*, 79.

tices and relations with humanity and the world around them with regard to how they understand their religious observance.

Let the reader not miss the critical difference between religion and the observance of religion – the former is what God has prescribed, while the latter is the application of humanity to these norms and practices, and there is a great gulf between them. Ignorance of this critical distinction has led many objectors to deny the validity of the said phrase, remaining adamant in their opposition to the expression.

Now, religion may be used to refer to its basic foundations and it may be used to refer to its perfections. Which of the two, then, is intended when we say that humanity is naturally prior to it?

The answer is that the basis of humanity is prior to the basis of religion, just as the perfection of the former is prior to the perfection of the latter, and this will become clear when we talk of the respects in which humanity is prior to religion.

As such, the gist of the phrase "Humanity before religion" is that humanity is prior to religious observance and worship insofar as religious observance stands in need of humanity, but without humanity being a cause for its existence or being concomitant to it. Furthermore, this statement does not address whether humanity is beneficial without religion or not, nor does it address which of the two is more important; it simply highlights the way in which religious observance and worship, generally referred to as religion, depends upon the notion of humanity.

PRECEDENCE IN THE SCHOLARLY TRADITION

As we have explained it, the said phrase is neither new to the Islamic tradition nor is it an unprecedented invention which no other scholar has affirmed; rather, it is a fairly common notion.

One of the luminaries of Islamic thought, al-Ghazālī – may God grant him His Mercy – stated in *Mīzān al-ʿAmal*: "He [the Prophet] – may blessings and peace be upon him – said: 'There is no true belief for one with no shame,' because shame for humanity is among the first signs of the intellect, and true belief is the loftiest station of reason, so how can one reach the final station without passing the first?!"[19]

Al-Ghazālī also wrote:

> No one will reach [the first category of felicity, namely, the afterlife] except through achieving the second category of God's blessings, namely, individual virtues, which we have stated in general are contained in four virtues: (i) intellect and its perfection, that is, knowledge; (ii) restraint and its perfection, that is, scrupulousness; (iii) courage and its perfection, that is, struggle; and (iv) justice and its perfection, that is, benevolence; and [these four] are the true foundations of religion.[20]

It has already been mentioned that humanity is the collection of individual virtues, and if individual virtues as they are enumerated by al-Ghazālī are the foundations of religion itself, then humanity is the foundation of religion and precedes the notion of religion by necessity.

These two statements are even more explicit and more ambivalent with regard to the meaning that the detractors against the said phrase are concerned about; for these two statements affirmed that some virtues are prior to true belief in its foundation, and not merely prior insofar as man acquires them before true belief, as is the case in our phrase.

---

19.   al-Ghazālī, *Mīzān al-ʿAmal*, 164.
20.   Ibid., 178.

And before al-Ghazālī, al-Rāghib al-Iṣfahānī – may God grant him His Mercy – made a similar statement in his *al-Dharīʿah*, writing:

> If it is said: in what sense did the Prophet – may blessings and peace be upon him – state: "There is no true belief for one with no shame"? It is said: Shame is the first sign of intellect, and true belief is its final station, and it is impossible for the final station to obtain for one who has not obtained the first, so it is necessary that if one has no shame, then they have no faith.[21]

And he wrote elsewhere: "These virtues, when they are obtained ... humanity, freedom, and dignity are [also] obtained, and it is this basis which is the foundation of religious observance, true belief, fear of God, and sincerity."

Similarly, Rukn al-Dīn ʿAlāʾ al-Dawlah al-Simnānī (d. 736/1336) – may God grant him His Mercy – in his book *Tabyīn al-Maqāmāt wa-Taʿyīn al-Darajāt*, articulated over a hundred stations in the ascent of the seeker towards God. Within each station he mentioned a number of degrees. The first station he refers to is termed "censure (*rijz*)". Its first degree was that which occurs to the novice on the spiritual path when the self is censured against what conflicts with reason; the second is to censure the self against what conflicts with revelation; and the third is to censure it against being preoccupied with what is irrelevant to one's affairs.[22] Similarly, al-Simnānī's twenty-second station is that of refinement (*adab*) and also, for the novice, comprises three degrees. The first is for the seeker to refine himself with the norms of reason; the second is to refine himself with the norms of revelation; and the third is to refine himself with the norms of the supererogatory. Note how in

---

21.   al-Rāghib al-Iṣfahānī, *al-Dharīʿah*, 208.
22.   al-Simnānī, *Tabyīn al-Maqāmāt*, 69.

both cases al-Simnānī gave priority to the demands of reason over the demands of revelation in emptying oneself of vice in the station of censure, and the demands of reason in adorning oneself with virtue as in the station of refinement.

Imam Burhān al-Dīn Ibrāhīm ibn ʿUmar b. Ḥasan al-Biqāʿī (d. 885/1480) in his exegesis of the Qurʾanic chapter "The Ants", when discussing the section on the people of the prophet Lūṭ – may peace be upon him – writes: "The secret behind his [Lūṭ's] calling them merely to abandon lewdness as opposed to polytheism, despite the fact that they were polytheists, is because he saw that they had descended to the level of animal-ity, so he approached them by calling them first to humanity, and from there, to the level of divine unity."[23] This twofold approach is exactly the explicit approach that is contained in the priority of humanity to religion.

Niʿmatullāh ibn Maḥmūd al-Nakhjuwānī, known as Shaykh ʿAlwān (d. 920/1514), wrote the following in his exegesis: "Who-ever does not ascend … above the rank of animality and has not reached the lofty rank of humanity … then the tree of his being and appearance will not bear the fruit of knowledge and certainty … for the sake of which it was planted to begin with."[24]

Finally, as in the words of Imam ʿAbdullāh ibn ʿAlawī al-Ḥaddād (d. 1132/1720) – God have mercy on him and benefit us by him:

> Indeed, whenever a man falls short of the rank of humanity, as in being overpowered by his desires or his passions, so strongly that he loses his composure, then he becomes an animal with respect to what has over-taken him; because every animal wherein one of these

---

23. al-Biqāʿī, *Naẓm al-Durar*, 8:174. What is cited here is one of two possibilities that al-Biqāʿī entertains in discussing why our master Lūṭ – may peace be upon him – sufficed with calling his people to refrain from lewdness, and the entire discussion will be cited in full in the sixth aspect of priority below.
24. al-Nakhjuwānī, *al-Fawātiḥ*, 1:280.

attributes overtakes the others is thereby known by it,
so if one of these attributes overpowers one among the
children of Adam, then by default he is attributed to the
animal that is characterized primarily by it.

So if one is overtaken by gluttony that person is
often referred to as a pig for the pig is considered a glut-
tonous species in the kingdom of animals.

Therefore, if one seeks to reach God, one needs to
struggle against oneself until one reaches the degree of
humanity first, and that is the rank of what is unique
to humanity to the exclusion of all other animals; it is
from there and *only* from there that one then continues
to struggle until one reaches [God]."[25]

Or take the consideration Muḥammad Anwar Shāh al-
Kashmīrī (d. 1353/1933) – may God grant him His Mercy – puts
forward in his commentary on al-Bukhārī's hadith compilation:

Know that some noble virtues which are principles for
true belief are considered prior to it, and are dyed with
the colour of true belief, such as integrity (*amānah*),
and that is why he [the Prophet] said: "The one without
integrity does not have true belief," for integrity is prior
to true belief, and it is incumbent to judge that shame is
prior to it as well.[26]

Lastly, among contemporary scholars we find Shaykh
Abdullah Bin Bayyah – may God preserve him – stating: "Human dignity is prior in conception and existence to the dignity
of true belief."[27]

If one sought to exhaust the statements of the scholars on
this question, they would certainly discover a great deal of

---

25. al-Ḥaddād, *Tathbīt al-Fu'ād*, 1:37.
26. al-Kashmīrī, *Fayḍ al-Bārī*, 1:153.
27. Bin Bayyah, "Taʿrīf al-Akhar bayn al-Falsafa wa-l-Islam," http://binbayyah.net/
     arabic/archives/4146.

corroborations, and we shall suffice here with the examples given from a vast array of scholars over several centuries up to and including our current age.

THE RELATIONSHIP BETWEEN HUMANITY AND RELIGIOUS OBSERVANCE

We have previously discussed that the meaning of humanity is to be considered an individual quality and virtue, and on that basis we defined it as distinct to religion. "Religion" here refers to the general meaning of religion as religious observance. That is because religious observance is an action while virtues are qualities, but they have a relation of conditionality or causal dependence, as we shall clarify in the section on the different ways that humanity is prior to religious observance.[28]

By explaining previously that humanity and religious observance are distinct, it becomes clear that nothing prevents the obtaining of the quality of humanity to one with no religion. Moreover, this assertion is not undermined from what may be understood from some verses of the Qur'an which seem to negate the humanity of those without religion, such as verses which compare disbelievers to cattle and so on, because these verses do not serve to negate the reality of humanity from them and instead are only a caution against not achieving the true purpose and fruit of humanity as a virtue. That is, the purpose of one's humanity is that it leads one to religious observance and knowledge of God, and that is the greatest aim in bestowing man with that humanity by which the human being is distinguished from all other animals. Now, since religious observance is the ultimate aim of humanity, as we know, it remains logically possible to negate humanity from one who

---

28. Humanity can also denote acting in a noble way but only figuratively in the sense that it is a cause of noble action, though that is not what is meant in our context.

has no religion, not because they do not have humanity, but because it has not led its agent to his ultimate aim, so it is as if he did not have it.[29] This is because "for everything that is created for a particular action, whenever that action does not occur from them, then that thing is treated as nonexistent."[30] On this basis, it is possible to negate humanity as an intrinsic value within a person.[31]

THE VARIOUS WAYS IN WHICH HUMANITY IS PRIOR TO RELIGION

The number of ways in which humanity is prior to religion is in proportion to the external referents of humanity and their variations in priority over religion. It has been shown that humanity is receptive to being true of each one of the virtues unique to mankind, and with respect to each human virtue which is prior to religion, it becomes manifestly clear to us one way among many in which humanity is prior, that is, insofar as it is true of that one particular virtue. We turn to examine in more detail some of the most important aspects of humanity which reveal its priority over religion.

(1) Acquiring Religion in Practice Is Dependent on the Acquisition of Humanity as a Trait

The basic foundation of religion cannot be obtained when there is an absolute absence of humanity. As such, it is in proportion to what one obtains for a human being that they are able to advance in the stations of religion.

---

29. See al-Rāzī, *al-Tafsīr al-Kabīr*, 32:339, on the verse "and you see the people enter God's religion in waves" (Q110:2).
30. al-Rāghib al-Iṣfahānī, *Tafṣīl al-Nash'atayn*, 80.
31. This form of expression is very common in the Arabic language, and the linguist Ibn Fāris (d. 395/1004) dedicated a chapter to this form of expression in his al-Ṣāḥibī with the heading "On Negating Something in Its Entirety Due to the Incompleteness of Its Qualities".

Now, the basic dependence of religion on humanity will repeat in each phase of religion: (1) knowledge; (2) belief; and (3) practice. Here we provide a short summary of this.

The Phases of Entry into Religion

As for the first phase, it is inconceivable for one to enter religion and believe in it without having knowledge of the validity of that religion first and grasping its truth. This is apparent, since it is not possible to believe in something that is unknown, nor even to reject it, for what is unknown cannot be the object of knowledge let alone of belief. Therefore, knowledge of the truth of religion and its validity is the first condition for the possibility of entry into religion.

Once the agent has grasped the truth of the Prophet, he must submit to what he has come to know is truth. So long as his intellect accepts that truth but he remains unhappy to submit to what he has believed, he remains in a state of obstinacy, which God describes as: "Verily they are not denying you, but rather, the transgressors are in denial of God's signs" (Q6:33). Thus, it is clear that after rational belief and assent to its truth, one must acquire an acceptance of the heart which the scholars of *kalām* describe as the very self's internal speech proclaiming, "I have believed and accepted." This is the second phase.

After the acceptance of the heart and soul of what the mind has grasped, there remains the drive of the heart and body towards acting on what they have accepted, both the inward assurance of the self, and the outward acts of worship. This is the third phase. This no doubt a part of the perfection of true belief, and also a part of its foundation, if we consider the position that holds that actions are a condition for the obtaining of true belief.

God Most High indicated this three-phase development of the seeker of divine guidance in the Qur'an by stating: "Let those who have been given knowledge know that this is the truth from your Lord, so let them believe in it, and let their hearts submit to it" (Q22:54).[32] Therefore, after knowledge comes assent, and that is true belief (*imān*). Then comes action, referred to here with the term "*ikhbāt*" (submission), which is action over and above mere belief.

The Dependence of Each Phase on Humanity

Now that you have conceived of the phases of true belief and entry into religion, which are the first two steps of religious observance, I now present to you how each of these phases is dependent upon the notion and trait of humanity:

As for the dependence of the first phase, namely, knowledge of the religion, it relies on the fact that the means to acquiring knowledge of the truth of religion is to consider what the Prophet – may blessings and peace be upon him – has brought forward, and to reflect on its evidences and the miracles which he has come with until that person, the moral and rational agent, is guided by means of his intellect to the fact that these statements can only truly come from God. As for the agent who does not even listen to the message, or one who listened to it in an unreflective sense, such that he did not bother to consider the signification of the signs which indicate the truth of prophethood, then he will never come to know whether the claims of the prophets are true. Reflection is an absolute condition for the obtainment of knowledge.

Many scholars have investigated among themselves what it is that drives the moral and rational agent to search, reflect, and consider all that might reveal to him the truth of prophethood.

---

32. The full verse is: "Let those who have been given knowledge know that this is the truth from your Lord, so let them believe in it, and let their hearts submit to it, and their hearts may be made humbly [open] to it – for verily God is the Guide of those who believe, to the Straight Way."

After considering the possibilities and reflecting on them, they concluded that what drives one to reflection – as stated by the scholars of *kalām* – is the motivational nature of man, which gives rise to anxiety in the agent when he hears of punishment and reward, and tasks him to think and verify the truth of a claimant's claims or falsehood therein. For, as al-Ghazālī states:

> Reflection is a cause in knowing truth, and the intellect is the instrument of reflection and understanding of the meaning of the information and reports it is confronted with. And the motivational nature of humans calls them to be heedful after they have understood the danger [of something] using reason. Therefore, there must be a natural quality which is repulsed by the promise of punishment, and is attracted by the promise of reward, in order for it to be a motivator.[33]

This indicates to us that an agent whose inquisitive nature has been silenced or exterminated will be undisturbed when he hears of threats and punishment for the abandoning of reflection and belief, and therefore, will not seek to find the truth behind these claims.[34] From here we see how the hard-hearted and insensitive types are the furthest from the acceptance of religion and being affected by it, and this will be explained further in the discussion of the third way in which humanity is prior to religion.

---

33. al-Ghazālī, *al-Iqtiṣād*, 242–43.

34. This is indicated in the statement of 'Alī ibn 'Abdullāh ibn 'Abbās: "Whoever does not deem ignorance to be a deficiency, nor does he find the humiliation of sin in his heart, nor does he consider the error in his own speech when transgressing his limit against his opponent … then we do not expect such a person to abandon error, nor his incapacity to be removed, nor will he struggle to distinguish between proof and erroneous doubts." The relevance of this statement is that the one whose base attributes have rendered him void of feeling and sensitivity is no longer able to distinguish between proof and specious argument and does not struggle to distinguish them, and more shall follow on this statement in the next few pages.

Now, this degree of humanity, through the agent's inquisitive nature, has been granted to every rational agent. Therefore, the humanity of one which escapes the corruption of heedlessness shall answer the call by nature and reflect; and whoever refuses in obstinance shall be reckoned with for their shortcoming. It is thus clear in what sense the first phase of true belief, namely knowledge of the religion, is dependent on humanity; that is, it is dependent on it insofar as knowledge is dependent on reflection, and the condition for reflection is to have this natural motivation which, in turn, requires a certain degree of humanity.

There is yet another aspect by which reflection is dependent on humanity, and that is with regard to the obstructions to reflection: such as arrogance, conceit, and fanatical or irrational attachment to the beliefs of one's own social or cultural group. Thus, the one engaged in reflection must have a certain degree of humility in order for him to reflect on what has been presented to him and, furthermore, he must reflect sincerely, such that he can truly grasp the truth. This is a part of one's humanity, and in this additional sense, knowledge of religion is dependent on humanity. Hence, knowledge of the truth of religion is dependent on one's humanity, and it is therefore prior to religion in these two respects.

As for the dependence on humanity of the second phase – which is again belief and assent to what they have been guided to by means of reflection and acquisition of knowledge – then it is so insofar as it needs a fair degree of humility and sincerity to drive one to assent and accept the truth, and further, to combat one's egotistical desires. For one who possesses no humility at all, not even a little, it is inconceivable for such a person to take the lead of another person, even if the proofs are established against him that this person is sent by God the

Exalted and Supreme, and that is why arrogance is the greatest of all obstructions to answering the call of God's messengers.

This degree of humility which assent requires is greater than what is needed for reflection, for an arrogant person may not have so much arrogance that it would prevent him from even thinking or reflecting, but he will never concede and accept what he knows to be true. The vice of arrogance will diminish any form of receptivity for the truth of any claim or statement. Indeed, God has revealed how He distances the arrogant man from submission to what he knows to be true in the clearest and most emphatic way: "I shall divert from My Signs those who are arrogant in the Earth without any right, and if they see every sign they shall not believe, and when they see the path of guidance, they will not advance upon it, and when they see the path of misguidance they advance. That is because they have denied Our Signs and were heedless of them" (Q7:146). This dependence of true belief on the absence of arrogance and ultimately on humanity was also indicated by Yūnus ibn ʿUbayd (d. 140/757)[35] – may God grant him His Mercy – when he said, "In this community [of the Prophet Muhammad] there is no pure ostentation nor pure arrogance." So, he was asked "Why is that?" He said: "There is no arrogance with prostration, nor ostentation with belief in God."[36] This indicates the need for some degree of humanity which manifests itself in

---

35. Ibn Dīnār, the great imam and exemplar, the proof, Abū ʿAbdullāh al-Baṣrī. He was among the younger generation of Successors and their elites. Ghassān ibn al-Mufaḍḍal al-Ghallābī said: "It was reported to me by some Companions, who said: 'A man came to Yūnus ibn ʿUbayd and complained of his circumstances and livelihood and his depression, so he said to him: "Would you accept 100,000 [dinars] for your sight?" He said: "No." "And your hearing?" "No." "And your speech?" "No." "And your intellect?" "No." And he kept reminding him of God's blessings then he said: "I see you have hundreds of thousands, and yet you complain of need?"'" Abridged from al-Dhahabī, *Siyar Aʿlām al-Nubalā'*, 6:384.

36. al-Shaʿrānī, *Lawāqiḥ al-Anwār*, 1:31.

humility and sincerity, by which a human being may enter into the community of acceptance.

The aforementioned scholar al-Nakhjuwānī likewise asserted the dependence of certainty and true faith on the existence of humanity in his commentary on the Qur'an, writing the following:

> It is clear to the hearts of deep insight into the core of divine unity, beyond its mere outer shell, that whoever does not rise – among those who embark upon the path of guidance in seeking God – above the rank of animality and does not reach the lofty rank of humanity, then the tree of his being and appearance will not bear the fruit of knowledge and certainty … for the sake of which it was planted to begin with.[37]

As for the dependence of the third phase (which is practising what one has believed in one's heart) on humanity: that is due to its dependence on a certain degree of humility, discipline against egotistical desires, and the ego's natural longing for the immediate pleasures of the world. Here, the amount required of this is greater than the amount required for mere assent. Many people may submit to the Shari'ah against the desires of their ego and in denial of its temptation to reject it; but they may be unable to overpower their desires which prevent them from performing acts of obedience.

We can confidently conclude that religious observance requires a certain receptivity and sensitivity to the Discourse of God the Exalted, and to be affected in this way is dependent on kindling the tinder of humanity in the subject of that Discourse. Reflect on the statement of the Real, the Transcendent: "Verily, in that there is a reminder for whoever has a heart" (Q50:37).

---

37. al-Nakhjuwānī, *al-Fawātiḥ*, 1:280.

Whoever's heart has ossified and turned to stone such that it does not tremble at any threat, nor does it long for any promise, nor is it enslaved by acts of benevolence, nor is it hurt by acts of harm, nor does it take pleasure in beauty, nor is it repulsed from the hateful and hideous, then how shall the exhortations, signs, and parables of the Qur'an and the Prophet – may blessings and peace be upon him – have any way to his heart, when all the channels of his hearing seem to have been firmly locked? And what good will it do for one to listen to the enumeration of God's blessings of which He reminds mankind constantly, if one has been stripped of all sensitivity and indebtedness to the One who has blessed one?

(2) Religion Has Come to Perfect Humanity

Humanity occupies a noble place among the aims of the divine messages and the missions of the prophets, and in this regard the Prophet Muhammad – may peace and blessings be upon him – said: "I have only been sent to perfect noble character."[38] This entails that the perfection of noble character is thereby a kind of final cause, and according to the rules of logic we know that a [final] cause is prior to its effect in the mind, even if it is posterior to it in existence and occurrence. This kind of priority is sufficient to let us reiterate the natural priority which noble character takes over religion in the sense that religion is there to perfect the virtue which we called humanity. Since humanity as a virtue existed and exists prior to the Prophet's mission, such that the mission has been decreed in order to perfect what is missing in humanity, and to rebuild what had been destroyed of it, evidently, this includes the idea that the prophetic mission is prior to religious observance and, thereby, humanity as a virtue is something that exists prior to religion.

---

38.   See Mālik, *Muwaṭṭa'*, #3357; Aḥmad Ibn Ḥanbal, *Musnad*, #8952.

For what is prior to something that is prior to another is also prior to that thing.

The great writer al-Rāfiʿī (d. 1356/1937) related this idea brilliantly in his description of the advent of religion to protect humanity and repair its foundations when he said:

> The Adamic meaning in this humanity, as if due to the duration of time, becomes eroded, and it is infiltrated by evil. So God intervenes in the history of mankind by sending forth a new Adam, with whom the world began in its highest evolution by means of which man is elevated, just as man began his existence in himself. And so humanity, for all time, is between two paths: one of them is the opening of the path of descent from the Garden, and the second is the opening of the path of return to the Garden. In Adam there is the secret of the existence of humanity, and in Muhammad – may peace and blessings be upon him – the secret of its perfection.
>
> That is why the religion propagated by the Prophet Muhammad is called *al-Islām*. Within the term lies the submission of the self to its obligations, that is, to its reality in social life, as if the Muslim denies himself and presents his ego to humanity in order to administer its affairs, perfect it, and elevate it. And so there is no share for the one who restrains himself against [the ego's] desires and individual gains, but rather, the shares are for humanity.[39]

Al-Rāghib al-Iṣfahānī interpreted God's sending of the prophets as one way among many for the protection of humanity:

> Whenever people abandon the practice of benevolence, magnanimity, and justice among themselves, such that they are void of it in themselves and in their actions,

---

39. al-Rāfiʿī, *Waḥy al-Qalam*, 2:97.

then if there remains in them some effects of goodness, God raises among them one who will guide them with speech and the just sword, such as the sending of the Prophet – may peace and blessings be upon him – to the Arabs, on account of what remained among them of goodness, such as glorifying the sacred month, the holy house, and the upholding of promises.

And if there remains very little receptivity to good, then God appoints one to dominate them with the sword of wrath, as God says: "And as such we appoint some of the transgressors to rule over others on account of their actions" (Q6:129). And He deals with them as He dealt with the Israelites when He sent Nebuchadnezzar, and God mentioned this in His statement: "When Our promise came to the first of the two, We sent against them Our servants, men of great strength in warfare, and passed through their residences, and God's promise was fulfilled" (Q17:5).

And if there remains no receptivity, God sends them a punishment that annihilates them, such as the flood, or the cry, or a blazing flame, or a terrible wind, or locusts, lice, frogs, and blood, to purify the lands of them, and relieve God's servants, just as God had done with the people of ʿĀd, Thamūd, the people of Nūḥ, and the people of Lūṭ; so just as when the earth is covered in thorns and thickets, it must be cleared completely, and it is therefore lit in flames to return to its original state.[40]

Thus, since the welfare of humanity is one of the purposes of the prophets and of religion itself, it is therefore also one of the aims of the acts of worship and divine laws. We find ample examples within the texts of the sacred law affirming that the purpose of the acts of worship and other laws is to refine character and perfect human beings. Thus, one who reflects

---

40.   al-Rāghib al-Iṣfahānī, *al-Dharīʿah*, 2:127. In this connection, see also what was cited by Shaykh Muṣṭafā Ṣabrī Efendi, as a quote from Shiblī Nuʿmānī, in his *Mawqif al-ʿAql*, 4:52ff.

on the works on the meanings of divine legislation (Shariʿah) will witness a multitude of discussions on the purposes of the law in connection with the virtues.

(3) The Basis of Legislation in Humanity

What we mean here is that divine legislation is built with the aim to serve human welfare, such that the laws conform to the requirements of unadulterated human nature. This is such that whenever humanity is blemished in an individual human being, the divine legislation calls for it to be protected and restored by dispersing all the sources and causes that accept or bring into existence such a blemish. The wisdom behind this is that the human being is the one who receives the content of revelation, so just as a deficiency in the receiver obscures the clarity of the signal and the manifestation of the beauty of the image, making it appear muddled and blurred, even if the sending device is functioning perfectly, the corruption of the soul likewise obscures the appearance of the beauty of revelation and the light of the noble law, so the various divine legislations manifest to their receiver in a manner that is repulsive, unclear, and disliked, even if the effects of revelation and its transmission of guiding lights is strong.

Indeed, this is what God indicates in His Book when He says: "And We reveal of the Qurʾan what is a cure and a mercy for the believers, and it does not increase the oppressors in nothing but loss" (Q17:82). And the Exalted says: "And when a chapter is revealed, there are some of them who say, 'Has this increased any of you in belief?' As for those who believe, it increases them in belief and in it they take solace. As for those with an affliction in their hearts, it increases them only in squalor, and when they die, they die as disbelievers" (Q9:124–25).

Commenting on this verse, Fakhr al-Dīn al-Rāzī (d. 607/1210) writes the following:

The meaning of *rijs* (squalor) is either their false beliefs or their vices, and if it is the second, the meaning [of the verse] is that they were afflicted with envy, enmity, and with acquiring new modes of deceit and wickedness, and now those vices have increased by virtue of the revelation of this new chapter.

The conclusion is that the soul which is purified from the love of the world, and is attributed predominantly with the love of God and the afterlife, listens to this chapter, and its listening leads to the increase of its desire for the afterlife and its repulsion from the world. As for the soul which is covetous of this deteriorating world for its own sake, seeking out its pleasures, in heedlessness of the love of God and the afterlife, when it hears this particular Qur'anic chapter, which speaks of *jihād*, subjecting one's life to negative things such as the chance of being killed in battle, or giving away one's wealth, it intensifies its disbelief.[41]

The great scholar Shaykh Muḥammad Mutawallī al-Shaʿrāwī (d. 1419/1998) – may God grant him His Mercy – commented on this verse by stating, "the health of one's human nature or its corruption has a strong effect on one's receptivity to the Qur'an."[42] Thus, if one's nature is sound, and the self is free of negative qualities, it becomes capable of witnessing the lights and beauties of revelation. Otherwise, those lights will be prevented by the darkness. This is what it means for revelation and divine legislation to be built on humanity; in other words, revelation aims at effecting and guiding those of sound human dispositions. This is why you see the reversal of its effects when one's human nature is unsound.

Similarly, Ibn al-Najjār al-Ḥanbalī (d. 972/1564) points to the foundational role for humanity with respect to revela-

---

41.   al-Rāzī, *al-Tafsīr al-Kabīr*, 16:174.
42.   al-Shaʿrāwī, *Tafsīr al-Shaʿrāwī*, 14:8711.

tion and divine legislation when analysing the question of the intrinsic good and bad (*al-taḥsīn wa-l-taqbīḥ al-ʿaqliyayn*):

> Ibn al-Qāḍī al-Jabal said: "Our shaykh said – meaning the Shaykh Taqī al-Dīn – and others: 'The good and the bad are real, and obligation and prohibition obtain through the [divine] command, and punishment is contingent upon sending prophets; and the normative good and bad are reducible to conformity and repulsion [of human nature]; because the normative good comprises praise and reward, which conform, while the normative bad comprises blame and punishment, which repulse.'"[43]

Likewise, al-Ṭāhir Ibn ʿĀshūr (d. 1393/1973) stated the following in his exegesis of the Qurʾanic verse "O Children of Adam, We have given you garments and feathers to clothe your vulnerabilities" (Q7:26): "This is an indication that clothing is rooted in the basis of human nature, and human nature is the first foundation of Islam."[44] Since the foundation is prior to the branch by nature, then it is prior to religion.

(4) Giving Life to the Form of Religion

The difference between this sense of priority and the first and the third is that the first shows the dependence of the existence of true belief on the existence of some degree of humanity, while the third shows the dependence, receptivity, and consonance between divine legislation and humanity. This shows the dependence on humanity of the efficacy of religious observance on the agent after his applying those norms.

Imam Jamāl al-Dīn Muḥammad ibn ʿAbdullāh ibn Shaykh al-ʿAydarūs (d. 1031/1622) – may God grant him His Mercy – notes:

---

43. Ibn al-Najjār al-Ḥanbalī, *Mukhtaṣar al-Taḥrīr*, 1:302.
44. Ibn ʿĀshūr, *al-Taḥrīr*, 8:74.

Among hearts there are some which God has freely made naturally incline to the good and naturally distance themselves from evil, and so, by their very nature they cohere with the good and are qualified by it. The possessors of such hearts are the people of proximity to God, and between them and righteous action there is a strong connection, so when they move towards good actions ... they find these actions to be easily within reach due to that relation that holds between them ... So you see the possessors of these hearts decorated with the effects of these actions with very little effort. Then there are hearts which naturally oppose good action, due to their coarse and harsh nature; the possessors of such hearts find great strain in striving to do good works, and despite their striving, their practices hardly have any enlightening effects on them, due to the opposition between their natures and the good, so they exert themselves in good actions, but their effects escape them.[45]

The fruits of religious observance are acquired in proportion to the quantity of humanity present in the religious agent, and the evidence for this is overwhelming and our lived reality testifies to its truth. Observe, for example, the religious practice of the *khawārij* (and devout religious practice was one of their most notable characteristics) which resulted in nothing other than physical exhaustion and the absence of rest. This was not caused by anything other than the decoupling of their religion from their humanity and what it entails of compassion, humility, shame, and magnanimity.

Al-Bukhārī reports via Abū Saʿīd al-Khudrī – may God be pleased with him: "While we were with the Messenger of God – may blessings and peace be upon him – and he was dividing the spoils, a man named Dhū Khuwayṣirah came to him, and he was from the men of Banū Tamīm, and said: 'O Messenger

---

45. Ibn Shaykh al-ʿAydarūs, *Īḍāḥ*, 62.

of God, be just!' So [the Prophet] said: 'Woe to you, and who will be just if I am not? Verily you have certainly met disaster and loss if I was not just.' So, 'Umar said: 'O Messenger of God, permit me to strike his neck!' He – may blessings and peace be upon him – said: 'Leave him, for he has companions whose prayers will belittle your prayers, and whose fasts will belittle your fasts, and your fasting [in comparison] to their fasting; they will recite the Qur'an but it shall not go deeper than their throats, and they will pass through the religion just as the arrow goes through its target.'"

Similarly, in another sound hadith mentioned in all six canonical hadith compilations it has been reported that the Prophet – may blessings and peace be upon him – said: "There shall appear at the end of time youthful men of shallow minds who repeat the words of the best of humanity. They shall recite the Qur'an but it does not go deeper than their throats, they shall pass through the religion just as the arrow passes through its prey so, when you meet them, kill them, for verily in killing them there will be a great reward with God on the Day of Judgement for those who have killed them."

In both prophetic narrations, there is an affirmation of worship performed by these people, and a negation of its goodness or blessing for them, and when one seeks out the cause of what has corrupted their religious practice, we find that it consists in the insolence with the countenance of the Prophet Muhammad – may blessings and peace be upon him and his kinfolk – as well as the despicable words uttered by the man in the first hadith, and the shallow minds of those in the second hadith. This is all connected directly with their loss of humanity. Now, this gives us an opportunity to reflect on how the appearance of religious practice invoked the anger of the Prophet when it was brought forward while separated from the qualities of humanity, compassion, and subtlety. To the extent that the Prophet – may blessings and peace be upon him – said: "Are you a subverter?" And he said: "Among you are repellents."[46]

Meanwhile, the appearance of disobedience does not earn such ire when it occurs for one whose heart has some share of love which is an entailment of his humanity, such that the Prophet – may blessings and peace be upon him – said: "Do not curse him! For by God, I have known that he loves God and His messenger."[47]

The exegetes have stated in their commentary on the verse "the unrefined desert nomads are worse in their disbelief and hypocrisy" (Q9:97) that God the Exalted is informing us that "their disbelief and hypocrisy is greater than the disbelief of the people in Medina because they are coarser and harsher",[48] and "because they are harsher of nature and coarser of heart".[49] And one of the subtler ways to explain the intensity is their distance from humanity as stated in the exegesis of al-Rāzī, that the ones described by the verse "are like savages".[50] Since humanity is a condition for the efficacy of religion, and religion without efficacy has no benefit, then humanity is therefore a

---

46. Al-Haythamī in *Majmaʿ al-Zawāʾid* said: "It was narrated by Aḥmad, al-Bazzār, and the narrators in Aḥmad are men of the authentic books." See ibid., 2:71, #2370; and in [the narration of] Abū Yaʿlah, see ibid., 72.

47. al-Bukhārī, and the complete narration is as follows: "On the authority of ʿUmar ibn al-Khaṭṭāb, that there was a man during the time of the Prophet (S) whose name was ʿAbdullāh, and he was known as Ḥamārā, and he would often cause the Prophet (S) to laugh or smile. The Prophet (S) had ordered him to be flogged for drinking, and so he was brought to him one day and flogged, so one man among the people said: 'May God curse him! How often is he brought for this!' So, the Prophet (S) said: 'Do not curse him, for by God I have known that he loves God and His messenger,'" and in the narration reported by Ibn ʿAbd al-Barr: "… Do not utter that, for he loves God and His messenger."

48. al-Wāḥidī, *al-Wasīṭ*, 2:519.

49. See al-Mārwadī, *al-Nukat*, 2:393; and Ibn ʿAbd al-Salām, *Tafsīr al-ʿIzz Ibn ʿAbd al-Salām*, 2:45.

50. al-Rāzī, *al-Tafsīr al-Kabīr*, 16:125.

condition for religion, and conditions are prior to what they condition, and therefore, humanity is prior to religion.

(5) Its Motivation and Engendering of Religious Observance

Whenever humanity is realized in someone, it moves them towards good and righteous action, and such a person hardly hesitates a moment to answer the call of truth if its signs became sufficiently and convincingly apparent to him. As long as humanity remains the first step that one takes on the path of worship and practice of the law of God, then whenever a person answers the call of his sound disposition, characterized by the qualities of nobility, he will find himself after that in the open space of religious observance and worship, seeking the rewards through all of its means, as if that person were a magnet of religious practice due to its force of attraction, and in this sense, humanity is the receiver of religion, because it is what permits its messages to arrive.

Ḥāfiẓ Ibn Rajab al-Ḥanbalī (d. 795/1393) – may God grant him His Mercy – reported in his *Jāmiʿ al-ʿUlūm wa-l-Ḥikam*, via al-Jarrāḥ ibn ʿAbdullāh al-Ḥakamī, who was the warrior of the Levant, that he said: "I shunned sinning out of shame for forty years, then I obtained scrupulousness." Others said: "I saw the baseness of sins, so I shunned them out of decency until they became unthinkable due to piety."[51]

Abū al-Suʿūd Muḥammad ibn Muḥammad al-ʿImādī (d. 982/1574) wrote the following in commentary on the Qur'anic verse "Would not man remember that We have created him and before that he was nothing?" (Q19:67): "'Would not man remember?': Among the remembrance intended here is reflection, and the use of the explicit noun despite being the expected place for a pronoun is to further emphasize that humanity itself

---

51   Ibn Rajab al-Ḥanbalī, *Jāmiʿ al-ʿUlūm*, 1:501.

is among the drivers of reflection in the affairs of creation, and which directs it away from the aforementioned statement."[52]

Several exegetes point out yet another subtlety that brings out clearly the driving force of humanity towards religion in the Qur'anic statement "If it is said to them, 'Believe as the people have believed ...'" The exegetes stated that here the term "the people" – on the assumption that the definite article here means the genus – refers to those who are "complete in their humanity".[53] Thus, the meaning is "Believe [just as those who have completed their humanity, as entailed by intellect and discernment]".[54] This interpretation brings together the fragmented discussions in interpreting the term "the people" on the assumption that the definite article indicates that the identity of the noun is known to the listener, for based on that, it would mean per "the statement of Ibn ʿAbbās – may God be pleased with them – that 'Believe just as the Companions of the Prophet – may blessings and peace be upon him – believed,' and the statement of others who said it meant 'Just as those among the Jews, such as ʿAbdullāh ibn Salām and his companions ...' for both interpretations are valid, for both groups have acted in the manner entailed by their humanity."[55]

Yet this does not mean that whenever humanity is present then by necessity it must become religious, such that if it were not present then religious observance would become absent. This is because humanity is not a complete cause for religion, but rather is strictly one of the most important motivators, drivers, and guides to religious observance, even if the latter does not manifest with the presence of humanity, because it

---

52. al-ʿImādī, *Irshād al-ʿAql*, 5:274; al-Qāsimī cites this passage in *Maḥāsin al-Taʾwīl*, 7:108; see also Ibn ʿAjībah, *al-Baḥr al-Madīd*, 3:352.
53. al-Zamakhsharī, *al-Kashshāf*, 1:63; see also al-Rāzī, *al-Tafsīr al-Kabīr*, 2:307; al-Bayḍāwī, *Anwār al-Tanzīl*, 1:46; al-Nasafī, *Madārik al-Tanzīl*, 1:51; Abū Ḥayyān, *al-Baḥr al-Muḥīṭ*, 1:110; al-Nuʿmānī, *al-Lubāb*, 1:356.
54. al-Rāghib al-Iṣfahānī, *Tafsīr al-Rāghib*, 1:102.
55. Ibid.

remains in need of other causes. That is why you find that among many disbelievers, who are rational human beings like the rest of us, there is no difference between them and others who are qualified by humanity, nor in the soundness of their intellects and emotions, and so their waywardness is only due to the deprivation of due grace and the means of guidance, so we ask God for safety and refuge.

Now, by virtue of what has been established regarding humanity's motivation of religious observance and its being a means to it, and means are prior to their aims, it becomes clear that humanity is prior to religion.

(6) The Soundness of Religion Is Relative to the Soundness of One's Humanity

Just as a building's construction is unsound when its foundations are unsound, and a punctured vessel cannot hold what is poured into it, likewise, religion itself is unsound if one's humanity is unsound, and nothing remains of religious observance so long as it finds holes in the vessel of its humanity from which it leaks until it is drained entirely, because humanity is the vessel of religion.

It is likewise its means of preservation and repository, so no matter how much one struggles in one's religious practice, collecting together every valuable and rare item among its treasures, if one do not have humanity in one's storehouse to protect what one has collected among the treasures of religious observance, then such practices are more likely to fall into the hands of thieves in the night, and its possessor shall not find any benefit in it on the Day he must stand before his Lord.

As reported by Abū Hurayrah, "The Prophet – may blessings and peace be upon him – said: 'Do you know who the bankrupt one is?' They said: 'The bankrupt amongst us is he who has no money nor wealth.' The Messenger of God – may blessings and peace be upon him – said: 'The bankrupt one among my community is the one who comes on the Day of Judgement with his prayers, his fasting, his alms, yet he comes having insulted someone, and slandered another, and unjustly taken the money of another, and spilled the blood of another, and struck another, so he is seated until one [wronged] man takes from his good deeds, and then another takes from his good deeds, until his good deeds are depleted, but others remain who have yet to take their rights from him, so he is made to take of their sins and they are stacked above him until he is hurled into the Fire.'"[56]

In the hadith reported by al-Ṭabarānī in his *al-Muʿjam al-Ṣaghīr* we read: "Every [undesirable] action has its penance except for the man of poor character, for whenever he repents from a bad action, he repeats it with greater severity."[57]

ʿAlī ibn ʿAbdullāh ibn ʿAbbās said: "Whoever does not deem ignorance to be a deficiency, nor does he find the humiliation of sin in his heart, nor does he consider the error in his own speech when transgressing his limit against his opponent ... then he is not one whom we expect to abandon error, nor his incapacity to be removed, nor will he struggle to distinguish between proof and erroneous doubts."[58]

Yaḥyā ibn Muʿādh said: "Poor character is a vice which nullifies all benefit from even a great deal of good action, while good character nullifies all harm even from a great deal of bad actions."[59]

The following narration further explicitly testifies to the conditioning of religious observance by sound human nature:

---

56. See al-Tirmidhī, *Sunan*, #2418, who said: "This narration is authentic." See also Aḥmad Ibn Ḥanbal, *Musnad*, #8029; Ibn Ḥibbān, *Ṣaḥīḥ*, #7359.
57. al-Ṭabarānī, *al-Muʿjam al-Ṣaghīr*, 1:333.
58. See al-Jāḥiẓ, *al-Bayān*, 1:85; al-Ābī, *Nathr al-Durr*, 1:299; Ibn ʿAbd al-Barr, *Bahjat al-Majālis*, 1:394; and many others, and the quote above is the version in Ibn ʿAbd al-Barr with slight additions from the former two sources.
59. al-Ghazālī, *Iḥyāʾ ʿUlūm al-Dīn*, 5:186.

"Shame is the structure of true belief, so when the structure of something is compromised, it deteriorates and collapses."

Reflect on the loss that afflicts the practising agent who is devoid of humanity, and how prosperous the possessor of humanity becomes even with a minimal amount of worship, in order to see how humanity is prior to religious practice. This is exemplified so clearly in the narration from Abū Hurayrah – may God be pleased with him – who said:

> It was said to the Messenger of God -- may blessings and peace be upon him – "Such-and-such a woman prays in the night, fasts during the day, yet in her speech she is harsh against her neighbours," so he said: "There is no good in her; she is in the fire." And it was said to him: "Such-and-such a woman prays the obligatory prayers only, fasts in Ramadan, and gives charity in dried yogurt, and does nothing else but harms no one." He said, "She is in the Garden."[60]

From this remarkable narration, it becomes clear that the quantity of one's acts of worship do not lead to benefit in the absence of humanity, but the abundance of humanity is beneficial with a minimal amount of worship, and that is the meaning of "Humanity before religion". And since humanity is a condition for the soundness of religion, and conditions are naturally prior to the conditioned, then humanity is prior to religion.

(7) The Priority of Humanity over Religion in the Call to Belief

This means that the revival of humanity through the discourse of the caller and his actions is prior to the call to religious observance. This is due to what has preceded, namely, the

---

60.　al-Tirmidhī, #682; see also Aḥmad Ibn Ḥanbal, *Musnad*, #1230.

dependence of religious observance on humanity, humanity's conduciveness to religion, and its being a means to it. Seeking means is prior to seeking the aims; whoever has no water [for ablution] cannot be asked to pray before seeking it out. Likewise is the case for all means and their ends. Still, this particular sense of priority is treated independently due to its importance and its distinction from the previous cases by demonstrating the effects of the prior forms of priority on the science or craft of calling others, and in prioritizing one's discourse with them.

This does not mean that the caller to God should not begin his efforts by exhorting others to acts of religion until his addressees have achieved all the attributes of humanity and reach its furthest limits, for this is clearly wrong-headed. But rather, the point is that humanity has an effect on how to order one's priorities in religious discourse, and that setting humanity forth before calling others to religious practice is a way to increase the receptivity of the addressees and aid the efficacy of the caller.

Furthermore, the basic degree of humanity which religious observance requires means that one should prioritize calling to it whenever it is lacking, while going beyond that should be in accordance with the entailments of people's welfare and the balance between the level of religious practice and the level of humanity, for what is necessary is prioritized over what is strictly an improvement, and so on.

This aspect of priority was present to the scholars in their understanding of the discourses of the prophets – may peace be upon them – to humanity, as Imam al-Biqāʿī demonstrates in his exegesis of the Qur'anic chapter "The Ants". He discusses the secret behind the absence of the call to belief in divine unity in the discourse of our master Lūṭ to his people. This element is not mentioned in what God has informed us of his call, as opposed to all the other prophets whose discourses with their people God has informed us of. All of them prioritized – before warning them against the various forms of oppression and sinning among them – the call to the belief in divine unity and the command to worship. Al-Biqāʿī explains this in a way that corresponds to what we have stated. He says – may God grant him His Mercy:

> What is noteworthy is that it did not occur in the story of Lūṭ – may peace be upon him – other than his prohibiting them from lewdness, so their state must have been lacking one of two things: either they did not affirm any partners with God, but when they invented this lewd action and insisted on its publicity, they were swiftly punished due to their disbelief in their prophet, as stated explicitly in the verse of "The Poets"; or, they were polytheists, but Lūṭ – may peace be upon him – when he saw that they had fallen to the ranks of animals, ordered his call to them first towards the rank of humanity, and from there to the rank of divine unity. This second possibility is indicated by God stating that He has destroyed them and all those who have disbelieved before them, and that the objects of their worship could not save them: "Is God better? Or what they associate with Him?"[61]

Likewise, the Prophet Muhammad – may blessings and peace be upon him – repeatedly stated the importance of human virtues before the divine laws and rites when he would explain religion to those who first heard of him. It is reported in the hadith of our master ʿAmr ibn ʿAbsa al-Sulamī – may God be pleased with him – that he said:

> I wanted to abandon the gods of my people during the days of ignorance ... so I asked about [the Prophet] and I found that he had been very subtle about his affair. So

______

61. al-Biqāʿī, *Naẓm al-Durar*, 8:174.

I approached him gently and entered, greeted him, and said to him, "What are you?" and he said, "A prophet." So I said, "What is a prophet?" and he said, "The messenger of God." So I said, "Who sent you?" and he said, "God the Exalted." [I said,] "With what has He sent you?" and he said, "To preserve family bonds, to protect life, to protect the roads, to crush the idols, and to worship God alone, associating no partner with Him."[62]

In the hadith of ʿAbdullāh ibn Salām – may God be pleased with him – he said:

When the Messenger of God – may blessings and peace be upon him – came to Medina, the people went out to greet him, and I was among them, and when I saw his countenance, I knew that it was not the face of a liar, and the first thing I heard him say was, "Feed the hungry, spread the peace, pray while the people sleep, and you will enter the Garden in peace."[63]

This noble prophetic guidance was inherited by the scholars – may God be pleased with them – and it manifested itself in their methods of training and education, such that the hadith scholars – may God be pleased with them – made the first narration that any student hears be the hadith of compassion, reported with "firstness" (*al-musalsal bi-l-awwaliyyah*), so that the student comes to know this foundational principle, and that he may "know that the basis of knowledge is mutual compassion, love, and connection, and not cruelty and exclusion".[64]

---

62. Aḥmad Ibn Ḥanbal, *Musnad*, #17016.
63. al-Ṭabarānī, al-Muʿjam al-Kabīr, #553. In al-Muʿjam al-Ṣaghīr there is an additional phrase: "and preserve family bonds" before the statement "and pray while the people sleep". See also al-Maqdisī, al-Aḥādīth, #403.
64. al-Kattānī, *Fihris al-Fahāris*, 1:93.

There are countless examples in the lives of scholars who preach of the prioritization of humanity and awakening the good natures of others over the teaching of religion. In the discourses of the shaykh and teacher al-Ḥabīb ʿUmar ibn Ḥafīẓ – may God preserve him – in addressing the dangers of following what is disseminated by mass media regarding what may be harmful to true belief and certainty and reliance on God:

> How can we close our eyes and pretend we do not see reality? Rather we see what is being disseminated in the ramblings of the degenerate media as if it were true. Thus, O rational one! O listener! O seer! O human! O Adamic agent! Before we say, "O Muslim, O believer!" [we say,] "O *human*, O *Adamic agent*: the call to God is better for you."[65]

The relevant passage is that the discourse here is directed to others insofar as they are human beings and Adamic actors before their religious observance, before their being believers or their being Muslims. This is what it means for humanity to be prior to religion in the call to God.

The preceding has discussed the priority of humanity in the discourse of preaching, and the same can be said in its prioritization in their actions, which is the widest path in making one's discourse effective. This is clear from the effectiveness of people's character on the souls of those being called, and that this effect becomes the key to being influenced by the acts of worship of the caller and their religious actions. This is abundantly clear from the life of the Prophet – may blessings and peace be upon him – and his calling of the polytheists with his very state of being and actions, which in turn became the

---

65. From the discourses of the shaykh explicating the commentary of Shaykh ʿAlī Barās on Ibn ʿAṭāʾillāh's *Aphorisms*, 29 November 2019. See http://alhabibomar. com/Lesson.aspx?SectionID=7&RefID=25720 (22:48).

bridge to true belief and adopting his religion. "Rationally speaking, the majority of them were tacitly convinced by the authenticity of Muhammad's prophethood, but [their conviction] was silenced by arrogance and a fanatical tribalism. God says, 'They denied it but their souls knew it was true, in transgression and in arrogance' [Q27:14]. Furthermore, their love for his exemplary virtues and ethics is what overcame their arrogance and tribalism, so they submitted to him due to what they knew was true of him before that."[66]

CONTENTIONS RELATED TO THE PRECEDING

[THE FIRST CONTENTION]

One may argue: the claim that humanity is prior to religion is based on the false assumption that humanity is separate from religion such that it were entirely distinct from it, but in reality what you call "humanity" among those praiseworthy attributes is in fact from the essence and core of religion, and so your claim is defeated. That is because the statement "Humanity before religion" becomes equivalent to the statement "part of religion is prior to religion", and this is a meaningless statement.

Furthermore, all of the praiseworthy qualities including what you call humanity are taken from the guidance of the prophets, and this was expressed by Imam ʿAlī ibn Muḥammad al-Ḥabashī (d. 1333/1927) – may God grant him His Mercy – in his unpublished *Mawlid*: "Every virtue that is praiseworthy in man is taken from the crown of existence." Thus, holding that humanity is distinct and prior to what is acquired from the prophets is misguided.

The answer: we do not concede that humanity is from the core of religion, due to what has preceded, namely, that humanity is a quality while religion is a series of actions, and

---

66. al-Būṭī, *Min Hunā wa-Hunāk*, 145.

therefore, it is inconceivable for one of them to be part of the other. It has also been shown previously that humanity obtains without religion, for it is entailed by human nature which all human beings partake in, and that is why it occurs for some disbelievers as well.

From this, the distinction between humanity and religion becomes clear and, therefore, it is not a part of it.

As for the claim that all praiseworthy virtues are taken from religion, then the response is to say that this is outside the scope of the dispute. This is because humanity can be decoupled from religion, such that it comes to exist as we showed earlier. And if the objector says, "It does not become separated from religion," this objection does not touch the claim, due to the distinction we have shown between religion (as beliefs and prescriptions) and religious observance.

As for the claim that all virtuous qualities are taken from religion, it is true if they mean that believers find all these qualities in religion and acquire them from it, and that it does not conflict with what religion exhorts people to enact. But if they mean by this that it is not possible for any human being in the world to be guided to the virtuous qualities of humanity unless they receive them from religion, then this is not true. This is because the natural disposition and sound reason guide one to religion, and so whoever has both has humanity, even if they had never heard of any religion at all, can acquire these qualities naturally and instinctively without seeking them out or by means of education. This is clear and needs no argument or clarification through citations of scholars because I do not believe that a rational agent would doubt something so clear. Nevertheless, here are some quotations in that vein:

Consider the statement of the Prophet – may blessings and peace be upon him – to al-Ashaj ibn 'Abd Qays: "'You possess two qualities loved by God: forbearance and poise.' He said, 'O Messenger of God, did I acquire them or did God make me so instinctively?' He said: 'Indeed, God had made you so by instinct.' He said, 'Praise be to God who had made me instinctively acquire two qualities loved by God and His messenger.'"[67] The explicit nature of this hadith in the obtaining of such virtues without religion leaves no need to cite the commentators.

In the hadith of Abū Sufyān and his encounter with the Byzantine emperor Heraclius, he said, "By God, if it were not for the shame of being detected, I would have lied about [the Prophet Muhammad]."[68] Ibn Ḥajar al-ʿAsqalānī (d. 852/1449) wrote in *Fatḥ al-Bārī*: "This indicates that they considered lying a heinous act either on account of a previous law or by means of custom."[69] Thus, he held that custom was akin to a previous law in its prohibition against lying.

Indeed, Badr al-Dīn al-ʿAynī (d. 855/1452) added a third possibility in his *ʿUmdat al-Qārī* for the origins of their virtues:

> This indicates that people affirmed the ugliness of lying during the period of ignorance. It has also been said that this is evidence for one who claims that the ugliness of lying is known by reason, and al-Kirmānī said: "This does not follow, because it is possible for its ugliness to be customary or acquired from a previous law." I say: rather, reason judges the ugliness of lying and that it is contrary to reason, and it has never been reported from any religion that it permitted lying.[70]

Ibn Ḥajar also wrote in his commentary on the Prophet's statement – may blessings and peace be upon him – "The best

---

67.   Abū Dawūd, *Sunan*, 4:357, #5225.
68.   al-Bukhārī, "On How Revelation First Began to Come to the Messenger of God (S)", #7.
69.   al-ʿAsqalānī, *Fatḥ al-Bārī*, 1:35.
70.   al-ʿAynī, *ʿUmdat al-Qārī*, 1:85.

among you in the period of ignorance are the best of you in Islam when they learn": "Their nobility in the period of ignorance was due to their virtuous qualities insofar as they conform to human nature, especially by virtue of attributing themselves to their ancestors who had such qualities. Then nobility in Islam became by virtue of those normatively praised qualities." Thus, he held that the praiseworthiness of those qualities originated in their conformity to human nature, and if they were exhausted by the law he would have said "praiseworthy by virtue of what remained of previous laws".

This was discussed exhaustively by Abū al-Ḥasan ʿUbaydullāh al-Mubārakfūrī (d. 1414/1993) in *Mirʾāt al-Mafātīḥ*, where he wrote:

> That is, whoever was of the noble tribes in the period of ignorance, and had the capacity to receive good counsel, excellent virtues, and supremacy among his peers, but was prevented by the darkness of disbelief and ignorance, just as gold and silver are contained within the ores mixed in the dirt, Islam was the same. Then they outstripped their peers due to their readiness and virtues when they acquired knowledge and true belief, and were purified by means of struggle against the soul through worship, just as gold and silver are purified.[71]

The Yemeni scholar al-Shawkānī (d. 1250/1834) – may God grant him His Mercy – wrote the following in his *Nayl al-Awṭār*:

> It has been established in the authentic narrations that "People are ores like the ores of gold, the best of them in the time of ignorance are the best of those in Islam when they learn." In this narration there is an affirmation of virtue in the time of ignorance whence there was

---

71. al-Mubārakfūrī, *Mirqāt al-Mafātīḥ*, 1:305.

no fear of God, and he judged them to be the best in Islam on condition that they learn their religion, but the mere learning is not the cause of them being the best in Islam, otherwise, there would be no meaning to considering them the best in the period of ignorance, and every scholar of religion would be among the best even if they were not the best among them in the period of ignorance. Nor is the cause of their virtue in Islam strictly the fear of God, otherwise, there would be no use to calling them the best in the period of ignorance. Thus, there is no doubt that this report indicates that the nobility of origin and virtue have a role to play in being superior, and the elite of a people are the virtuous among them even if that has no effect in the affairs of religion or after-worldly reward.[72]

[THE SECOND CONTENTION]

It may be said: it is clear that religion motivates its subjects to acquire noble virtues and fill their hearts with nobility, compassion, and all other qualities of humanity, and here there is no disagreement. Therefore, religious observance is prior to humanity by agreement, because it is the cause of its acquisition, and if that is so, then the claim that humanity is prior to religion is a contradiction in terms.

The answer: there is no contradiction between the two claims, because what is prior to humanity in religion is not the same as what religion yields of humanity. To clarify this, it is necessary for some degree of humanity to exist for the basic establishment of religion or for its perfection, as we elaborated earlier. Then, the religion that is preceded by that degree of humanity will lead its subject to preserve what they have of their humanity from being taken by the bandits of rampant desire, then acquiring a greater and more refined share of hu-

---

72.   al-Shawkānī, *Nayl al-Awṭār*, 5:99.

manity, such that this share of humanity is considered the fruit of religious practice, and therefore, humanity and religion both feed into one another such that "the human – which is their religion – as he ages, becomes more perfected in his humanity and conformity to the Shari'ah."[73]

A parallel to this is the relation between true belief and righteous action, for righteous action is a cause for the increase of the intensity of true belief, and the increase is in turn a cause for action. Thus, each of them is prior to the other but in a different respect, and taking note of such respects resolves all issues in this regard.

The upshot is that humanity is necessary for religious observance insofar as its existence is dependent on it, and further, that its efficacy is dependent on one's share of humanity. Meanwhile, religious observance is necessary for humanity to maintain its strength and growth, and if humanity does not find in its religious practice what will give it the secret of continuity and preservation, it shall descend to the plains of annihilation and corruption, and here there is no dispute:

> We have known that the reality of the soul is that the humanity of the individual cannot ascend, imagine, and become felicitous with the truest felicity, nor mourn the loftiest mourning, unless it lives in the beloved. Humanity in this world shall not be realized unless it lives in its natural prophet, the prophet of its righteous virtues and lofty ethics and its precise order, and where shall they find this greatest beloved, except in Muhammad and the religion (*dīn*) of Muhammad – may blessings and peace be upon him?[74]

---

73. al-Rāfiʿī, *Waḥy al-Qalam*, 2:93.
74. Ibid., 95.

It may be said: the problematic element in the statement "Humanity before religion" is not so much in the precise meaning of the term but in the negative consequences of abandoning such a phrase in the minds of its listeners. That is because it prepares them to accept Western humanism which is premised on replacing religion with humanism and sufficing with the latter over the former, and this is a dangerous matter of which one must be cautious. In order to protect people from being influenced by such claims it is better not to utter such statements.

The answer: is that such a fear about the preparation to accept Western humanism should entail – according to this objector – that one abstain from praising humanity in any way, or at least, abstain from praising it before qualifying it with religion even if it would be true to do so, and that is to prevent people from accepting the corrupt notion of humanism being promoted by the West.

However, before we accept such noble counsel, we must first ask ourselves: does humanity, in our cultural inheritance, possess a noble meaning which the scholars affirm, promote, glorify, and call others to, or not? And is the judgement that it is prior to humanity – in the senses we have explained – as elaborated and strengthened by their statements, true or not?

Perhaps the most readily available answer is what has preceded, namely, that humanity has a noble meaning in our tradition, and the judgement that it is prior to religion in the senses we have described is taken from the niche of the scholars. And since that is the case, then what could require us to deny this technical term, which is free of any defect, which we find in our culture and our technical vocabulary? And why would we be silent on this judgement which is true of humanity?

No doubt that what would require that – according to the objector – is to distance people from accepting another mistaken notion. But is it not obligatory on us, against such conceptual manipulation, to clarify their proper meanings in our culture and tradition, such that they become distinct from other notions, and to give people insight into how they should understand these meanings which are repeated in our tradition?

How have we allowed this obligation of lifting the confusion and manipulation of the term "humanity" to fall into the hands of Westerners, while denying our own concepts and remaining silent on explaining their proper meanings in accordance with what is in fact true of it in the discourse of the lawgiver and the discourses of the scholars – may God be pleased with them?

Furthermore, some Westerners have made this their banner which they have raised in their call to replacing religion with something called "ethics" instead of humanity. Shall we, then, reject ethics as well, and stop praising them or stop describing the conditions for the soundness of religious practice and the validity of acts of obedience under the claim that we are protecting people from accepting the Western notion of ethics and virtues which separate them from religion?

This superficial approach to dealing with concepts that have been manipulated have led its proponents to abstain from explicating the notion of *jihād* in Islam, its rulings, and its virtues, due to its manipulation and confusion with modern terrorism, thus one fears explicating its virtues and importance in religion, for it may lead laymen to accept its extremist interpretation which calls towards extremist groups. This approach is deeply misguided as you can see; rather, it is obligatory to clarify the virtues and nobility of *jihād* with its legal conditions. The same applies to the term "humanity"; it is obligatory to explicate its virtues and nobility and to describe it as it truly is, while explaining that it cannot be a replacement for religion.

From this it is clear that there is no reason that the misuse by Western thinkers of the concept of humanity should prevent us from calling to it, elaborating its importance and priority over religion in the way we have done so here. Otherwise, every incorrect use of a technical term which normally signifies a correct meaning would entail that we abandon that term or remain silent on what is in fact true of it, and in which case, all of our terms would be open to manipulation by others, for every time they infiltrate some of it, we abandon it to them, and retreat in humiliation.

Thus, it is imperative, with regard to the question of humanity – in its incorrect meaning, the one that is cut off from religion – for us to respond by clarifying its valid meaning and how that meaning is important in our religion; that it is prior to worship and religious practice in the senses we have discussed above; that, further, it leads to proper religious practice and is concomitant to it; and that this is the purpose of humanity, as we clarified above. Thus, humanity does not benefit its subject in the afterlife if it is not redoubled with valid religious practice, and so on. Thus, our statement that "Humanity is prior to religion" is nothing but a part of an explanation of the place of humanity in our religion, and so it is necessary along with all the other parts which, when combined, the picture of humanity in our religion is thereby completed.

Nor is mentioning these particulars, such as its being prior to religion, an act of negating its other aspects – like its being of no benefit without religion in the afterlife – such that one can object and say: it is necessary to mention all other parts related to humanity in order to prevent anyone from falling victim to those other false claims. This is because the expression was never meant for a discussion on humanism which the West is calling to, such that the speaker must qualify his statement in such a way as to prevent their listeners from accepting humanism. Rather, these expressions were mentioned in the context of cautioning those who claim religious practice while being void of humanity and its virtues, and who have debased the value of human life and suffering, and have become savages in the form of human beings, in the context of pointing out the deficiencies in their actions and that true religion has nothing to do with their actions. Thus, it is appropriate to mention the true descriptions of humanity in this context in relation to the relevant subject under discussion, although it may be appropriate to caution others regarding corrupted notions of humanity with something else. But in this case, the religious practice of the said speaker, and his exhorting others to religious practice, and his warning them against disbelief is more than sufficient to protect listeners from misconstruing the intention of the speaker into meaning he seeks to undermine the religion or replace it with something else.

[THE FOURTH CONTENTION]
It may be said: if we concede the meanings mentioned above regarding the priority of humanity over religion, there remains some ambiguity in the statement, such that it has required all these pages of discussion to remove that confusion, and therefore, the expression is not void of criticism even when its meaning is clarified, for it has been accepted that the intended meaning is insufficient for deflecting the criticism.

Thus, the more appropriate counsel to others is to avoid ambiguous statements, and to affirm statements which cannot be understood in a problematic sense. Thus, we can say, instead of "Humanity before religion", a statement such as "Virtue is the measure of religion", or something to that effect, so that no one is led to believe that humanity is superior to religion, and at the same time, they deliver the intended meaning.

The answer: the first is that the disputant's statement here indicates that they have accepted the validity of the intended meaning, for if the meaning itself was false, they would not say "One may imagine a false meaning" but rather that "The meaning of the statement is explicitly false." Thus, the objection here has shifted from stating that the phrase is false to the objection that the phrase is ambiguous, albeit sustaining valid meanings, and all this indicates that the difference here is minimal and the resolution is close at hand.

The second reply: even though the disputant here has claimed that the statement is ambiguous, it is not true that every ambiguity requires us to modify the statement. Indeed, sometimes ambiguity is necessary, for "it is not possible to prevent all expressions from the imaginations of children and the ignorant, and to expend one's efforts to prevent that which leads to powerless expressions, dullness of wit, and heaviness of tongue."[75] Therefore, the balance between the desired good from one's speech and the degree of ambiguity that the statement carries, and preferring one over the other, is something that is subject to a difference of opinion between scholars, and thus, the claims of some are not a proof against the others. Suffice it to say that al-Ghazālī himself did not shy away from it, nor did al-Rāghib al-Iṣfahānī, al-Biqāʿī, and all the other scholars whom we have cited here under the heading "Precedence in the Scholarly Tradition".

Furthermore, not all these pages came to eliminate the ambiguity, but rather they contain digressions and elaborations on its meanings, and an explanation of the proper intent, and I do not think anyone would disagree on the validity of these elaborations, as is clear to any reader.

As for the claim that the statement therefore is not void of criticism on the basis that the intended meaning is insufficient

---

75.   al-Ghazālī, *Iljām al-ʿAwām*, 131.

for deflecting the objection, then this is not the case. That is because the context of their statement "The intended meaning does not deflect the objection" is only meant to refer to statements where either the evident sense of the meaning is not intended while also lacking a contextual signifier that determines its proper meaning, where the context does not require some kind of ambiguity; or, when the statement is an unambiguous indicator for something other than the intended meaning. Outside of these two cases, the principle in question is not relevant, as verified by the great scholar Abū al-Mawāhib al-Ḥasan ibn Mas'ūd al-Yūsī (d. 1102/1691) – may God grant him His Mercy – in his treatise on the subject.[76] It is evident that the meaning of the expression does not contradict its outward sense, nor is it an unambiguous text of something else, such that someone can apply this principle. Rather, the intended meaning of the statement is indicated by it in a way that is equal to the other meaning, and further, it has won the necessary determination given the contextual signifiers before it and after it. This is in addition to the imperative to protect speech from rejection and interpret it in the most charitable way, and so on, such that even if it lacked a clear contextual determination, the said principle would not apply. That is because in this case, the expression supports the valid meaning in equal proportion to the other, and it is not a statement which evidently or unambiguously points to another meaning, as per al-Yūsī.

As for the claim that the statement "Virtue is the measure of religion" correctly signifies the intended meaning without ambiguity, then that is not true because such a statement does not extend to cover the case of humanity's priority in calling others, and its being one of the aims of revelation, and so on.

---

76. al-Yūsī, *Rasā'il.*

In conclusion, it is appropriate here to point out that the reason which demanded one to point out the priority of humanity over religious practice is what was caused by the actions of many of the claimants to religious observance and the over-zealous defenders of religion at the expense of human blood, and the debasement of human suffering, and the sacrificing of the rights of humanity in pursuit of their selfish pursuits and purposes, exacerbating conflicts, lighting the fires of war, rejecting every good in the lives of people, the dominance of ugliness, anger, and cruelty in their claims and their contrivances in affirming some prophetic norms in their exterior, while harming others, leading to a disfigured model for religious practice which drives people away from their Lord and distances them from taking His path.

This problem is not limited to the absence of certain virtues such that the resolution is found in merely pointing them out, but the problem is so deep that it has become a dominant sign for this group that has led to a complete emptying of the forms of outward practice from their beauty and dignity. There is no means of re-emerging from this except through awakening one's humanity, which comprises proper refinement, compassion, kindness to others, and so on, all of which lead one to self-awareness, gratitude, mercy, and so forth.

You are not in need of reminders regarding certain ethics in your interactions with others, but you are in the process of inducing a state in others that entails a relationship to God and human beings that motivates them to enter the religion with mercy, subtlety, humility, and refinement in their interactions with God and creation, such that whenever that state is cut off from worship, it does not bring forth anything except the opposite results. Indeed, of all species, humanity is best suited to reach this goal, which will become clear to the one who reflects on the reality and definition of humanity, as mentioned in the beginning of this text.

May God's blessings and peace be upon our master
Muhammad, his kinfolk, and his Companions.
Praise be to God, Lord of all the worlds.

REFERENCES

al-Ābī, Abū Saʿd Manṣūr ibn al-Ḥusayn. *Nathr al-Durr fī al-Muḥāḍarāt*. Edited by Khālid ʿAbd al-Ghanī Maḥfūẓ. Beirut: Dār al-Kutub al-ʿIlmiyyah, 2004.

Abū Dāwūd, Sulaymān ibn al-Ashʿath al-Azdī al-Sijistānī. *Sunan Abī Dāwūd*. Edited by Muḥammad Muḥyī al-Dīn ʿAbd al-Ḥamīd. Beirut: al-Maktabah al-ʿAṣriyyah, n.d.

Abū Ḥayyān, Muḥammad ibn Yūsuf al-Andalusī. *al-Baḥr al-Muḥīṭ*. Edited by Ṣidqī Muḥammad Jamīl. Beirut: Dār al-Fikr, 2010.

Aḥmad Ibn Ḥanbal, Abū ʿAbdullāh. *Musnad al-Imām Aḥmad*. Edited by Shuʿayb al-Arnaʾūṭ. Beirut: Muʾassasat al-Risālah, 2001.

al-ʿAsqalānī, Aḥmad ibn ʿAlī ibn Ḥajar Abū al-Faḍl. *Fatḥ al-Bārī Sharḥ Ṣaḥīḥ al-Bukhārī*. Beirut: Dār al-Maʿrifah, 1959.

al-ʿAynī, Badr al-Dīn Maḥmūd ibn Aḥmad. *ʿUmdat al-Qārī Sharḥ Ṣaḥīḥ al-Bukhārī*. Cairo: Dār al-Ḥalabī, 1940.

al-Baghawī, Ḥusayn ibn Masʿūd, and Muḥammad al-Nimr. *Maʿālim al-Tanzīl*. Riyadh: Dār Ṭaybah, 1987.

al-Bājūrī, Ibrāhīm ibn Muḥammad. *Ḥāshiyat al-Bājurī ʿalā Sharḥ al-ʿAllāmah Ibn Qāsim al-Ghazzī ʿalā Matn Abī Shujāʿ*. Edited by Maḥmūd al-Ḥadīdī. Jeddah: Dār al-Minhāj, 2016.

———. *Ḥāshiyat al-Bājurī ʿalā Matn al-Sullam al-Munawraq*. Edited by Muḥammad Rawtān. Cairo: Dār al-Salām, 2019.

al-Bayḍāwī, Nāṣir al-Dīn ʿAbdullāh ibn ʿUmar. *Tafsīr al-Qurʾān al-Karīm li-l-Bayḍāwī*. Cairo: Maktabat al-Jamhūriyyah, 1960.

———. *Anwār al-Tanzīl wa-Asrār al-Taʾwīl al-Maʿrūf bi-Tafsīr al-Bayḍāwī*. Edited by Muḥammad ʿAbd al-Raḥmān al-Marʿashlī. Beirut: Dār Iḥyāʾ al-Turāth al-ʿArabī, n.d.

al-Biqāʿī, Burhān al-Dīn Ibrāhīm ibn ʿUmar ibn Ḥasan. *Naẓm al-Durar fī Tanāsub al-Āyāt wa-l-Suwar*. Cairo: Dār al-Kitāb al-Islāmī, n.d.

al-Bukhārī, Muḥammad ibn Ismāʿīl. *Ṣaḥīḥ al-Bukhārī*. Edited by Muḥammad Zuhayr ibn Nāṣir al-Nāṣir [based on the Ottoman ʿĀmiriyyah print]. Cairo: Ṭawq al-Najāh, 2001.

al-Būṭī, Muḥammad Saʿīd Ramaḍān. *Min Hunā wa-Hunāk: Humūm min Qaḍāyā al-Sāʿah*. Damascus: Dar al-Fikr, 2013.

al-Dasūqī, Muḥammad ibn Aḥmad ibn ʿArafah. *Ḥāshiyat al-Dasūqī ʿalā al-Waḍʿiyyah*. Edited by Marʿī Ḥasan al-Rashīd. Damascus: Dār Nūr al-Ṣabāḥ, 2012.

al-Dhahabī, Shams al-Dīn Abū ʿAbdullāh Muḥammad ibn Aḥmad Qaymāz. *Siyar Aʿlām al-Nubalāʾ*. Edited by Shuʿayb Arnaʾūṭ. Beirut: Muʾassasat al-Risālah, 1985.

al-Ghazālī, Abū Ḥāmid. *Iḥyāʾ ʿUlūm al-Dīn*. 1st ed. Jeddah: Dār al-Minhāj, 2011.

———. *Iljām al-ʿAwām ʿan ʿIlm al-Kalām*. 1st ed. Jeddah: Dār al-Minhāj, 2017.

———. *Mīzān al-ʿAmal*. Jeddah: Dār al-Minhāj, 2018.

———. *al-Iqtiṣād fī al-Iʿtiqād*. Edited by Anas al-Sharafāwī. Jeddah: Dār al-Minhāj, 2019.

al-Ghursī, Muḥammad Ṣāliḥ ibn Aḥmad. *Badr al-Tamām fī Taḥrīr Muhimmāt Qaḍāyā ʿAqāʾid al-Islām wa-Huwa Ḥāshiyah ʿalā al-Musāmara fī Tawḍīḥ al-Musāyarah li-Ibn Abī Sharīf*. Amman: Dār al-Fatḥ, 2018.

al-Ḥabashī, ʿAlī ibn Muḥammad. *Samṭ al-Durar fī Akhbār Mawlid Khayr al-Bashar wa-Mā lahu min Akhlāq wa-Awṣāf wa-Siyar*. Edited by al-Ḥabīb Aḥmad ibn ʿAlawī al-Ḥabashī. N.p.: 2015.

al-Ḥaddād, ʿAbdullāh ibn ʿAlawī. *Tathbīt al-Fuʾād bi-Dhikr Majālis al-Quṭb al-Imām ʿAbdullāh ibn ʿAlawī al-Ḥaddād*. Compiled by Aḥmad ibn ʿAbd al-Karīm al-Ḥasāwī al-Shajār. Edited by al-Ḥabīb Aḥmad ibn al-Ḥasan ibn ʿAbdullāh al-Ḥaddād. Singapore: 1999.

al-Haythamī, Nūr al-Dīn ʿAlī ibn Abī Bakr. *Majmaʿ al-Zawāʾid wa-Manbaʿ al-Fawāʾid*. Cairo: Maktabat al-Qudsī, 1994.

Ibn ʿAbd al-Barr, Abū ʿUmar Yūsuf. *Bahjat al-Majālis wa-Uns al-Majālis wa-Shaḥdh al-Dhihn wa-l-Hājis*. Edited by Muḥammad al-Khawālī. Beirut: Dār al-Kutub al-ʿIlmiyyah, n.d.

Ibn ʿAbd al-Salām, ʿIzz al-Dīn ʿAbd al-ʿAzīz. *Tafsīr al-ʿIzz Ibn ʿAbd al-Salām*. Edited by ʿAbdullāh ibn Ibrāhīm al-Wahbī. Beirut: Dār Ibn Ḥazm,1996.

Ibn ʿAjībah al-Ḥasanī, Abū al-ʿAbbās Aḥmad ibn Muḥammad ibn al-Mahdī. *al-Baḥr al-Madīd fī Tafsīr al-Qurʾān al-Majīd*. Edited by Aḥmad ʿAbdullāh al-Qurashī Raslān. Cairo: Ḥasan ʿAbbas Zakī, 1998.

Ibn ʿĀshūr, Muḥammad al-Ṭāhir ibn Muḥammad. *al-Taḥrīr wa-l-Tanwīr (Taḥrīr al-Maʿnā al-Sadīd wa-Tanwīr al-ʿAql al-Jadīd min Tafsīr al-Kitāb al-Majīd)*. Tunis: al-Dār al-Tūnusiyyah li-l-Nashr, 1984.

Ibn ʿAṭiyyah. *al-Muḥarrir al-Wajīz fī Tafsīr al-Kitāb al-ʿAzīz*. Beirut: Dār Ibn Ḥazm, 2002.

Ibn Fāris, Abū al-Ḥusayn Aḥmad. *al-Ṣāḥibī fī Fiqh al-Lugha wa-Masāʾilihā wa-Sunan al-ʿArab fī Kalāmihā*. Edited by ʿUmar Fārūq al-Ṭabbāʿ. Beirut: Dār Maktabat al-Maʿārif, 2013.

Ibn Fūrak, Abū Bakr. *Mujarrad Maqālāt al-Shaykh Abī al-Ḥasan al-Ashʿarī*. Edited by Daniel Gimaret. Beirut: Dār al-Mashriq, 1987.

Ibn Ḥibbān, Abū Ḥātim Muḥammad Aḥmad al-Bustī. *Ṣaḥīḥ Ibn Ḥibbān*. Edited by Shuʿayb al-Arnaʾūṭ. Beirut: Dār al-Risālah, 1993.

Ibn Mājah al-Qazwīnī, Abū ʿAbdullāh Muḥammad ibn Yazīd. *Sunan Ibn Mājah*. Edited by Muḥammad Fuʾād ʿAbd al-Bāqī. Cairo: Dār Iḥyāʾ al-Kutub al-ʿArabiyyah wa-Fayṣal ʿĪsā al-Bābī al-Ḥalabī, n.d.

Ibn Manẓūr, Abū al-Faḍl Muḥammad ibn Mukarram ibn ʿAlī. *Lisān al-ʿArab*. Beirut: Dār Ṣādir, 1998.

Ibn al-Najjār al-Ḥanbalī, Taqī al-Dīn Abū al-Baqāʾ Muḥammad. *Mukhtaṣar al-Taḥrīr Sharḥ al-Kawākib al-Munīr*. Edited by

Muḥammad al-Zuḥaylī and Nazīh Ḥammād. Riyadh: Maktabat al-ʿUbaykān, 1997.

Ibn Nujaym al-Miṣrī, Zayn al-Dīn Ibrāhīm ibn Muḥammad. *al-Baḥr al-Rāʾiq Sharḥ Kanz al-Daqāʾiq*. 2nd ed. Cairo: Dār al-Kitāb al-Islāmī, n.d.

Ibn Rajab al-Ḥanbalī, Zayn al-Dīn ʿAbd al-Raḥmān. *Jāmiʿ al-ʿUlūm wa-l-Ḥikam fī Sharḥ Khamsīn Ḥadithan min Jawāmiʿ al-Kalim*. 7th ed. Edited by Shuʿayb al-Arnaʾūṭ. Beirut: Muʾassasat al-Risālah, 2001.

Ibn Shaykh al-ʿAydarūs, Jamāl al-Dīn Muḥammad ibn ʿAbdullāh. *Īḍāḥ Asrār ʿUlūm al-Muqarrabīn*. 4th ed. Damascus: Dār al-Sanābil wa-Dār al-Ḥāwī, 2018.

al-Ījī, ʿAḍud al-Dīn, and Saʿd al-Dīn al-Taftāzānī. *Sharḥ Mukhtaṣar Ibn al-Ḥājib*. Edited by Shaʿbān Ismāʿīl. 2 vols. Cairo: Maktabat al-Azhariyyah li-l-Turāth, 1973.

al-ʿImādī, Abū al-Suʿūd Muḥammad ibn Muḥammad ibn Muṣṭafā. *Irshād al-ʿAql al-Salīm ilā Mazāyā al-Kitāb al-Karīm*. Beirut: Dār Iḥyāʾ al-Turāth al-ʿArabī, n.d.

al-Jāḥiẓ, ʿAmr ibn Baḥr. *al-Bayān wa-l-Tabyīn*. Edited by ʿAbd al-Salām Hārūn. Cairo: Maktabat al-Khānjī, n.d.

al-Jāwī al-Makkī, ʿAbd al-Ḥaqq ibn ʿAbd al-Ḥannān. *Tadrīj al-Adānī ilā Qiraʾat Sharḥ al-Taftāzānī ʿalā Taṣrīf al-Zinjānī*. 1st ed. Edited by Ṣuhayb Mullā Muḥammad Nūr ʿAlī Bi-l-ʿĪd al-Jazāʾirī. Damascus: Dār Nūr al-Ṣabāḥ, 2015.

al-Jubbāʾī, Abū ʿAlī. *Kitāb al-Maqālāt*. Edited by Özkan Şimşek. Istanbul: Endülüs Yayınları, 2018.

al-Jurjānī, al-Sayyid al-Sharīf. *al-Taʿrīfāt*. Beirut: Dār al-Kutub al-ʿIlmiyyah, 1984.

al-Kafawī, Abū al-Baqāʾ Ayyūb ibn Mūsā al-Ḥusaynī. *al-Kulliyyāt*. Edited by Muḥammad al-Miṣrī and ʿAdnān Darwīsh. Beirut: Muʾassasat al-Risālah, 2012.

al-Kashmīrī, Muḥammad Anwar Shāh ibn Muʿaẓẓam Shāh. *Fayḍ al-Bārī Sharḥ Ṣaḥīḥ al-Bukhārī*. Edited by Muḥammad Badr ʿAlam al-Mīrtehī. Beirut: Dār al-Kutub al-ʿIlmiyyah, 2005.

al-Kattānī, Muḥammad ʿAbd al-Ḥayy ibn ʿAbd al-Kabīr ibn Muḥammad al-Ḥasanī al-Idrīsī. *Fihris al-Fahāris wa-l-Ithbāt wa-Muʿjam al-Maʿājim wa-l-Mashyakhāt wa-l-Musalsalāt.* Edited by Iḥsān ʿAbbās. Beirut: Dār al-Maghrib al-Islāmī, 1982.

al-Laythī, Abū al-Qāsim ibn Abī Bakr. *Ḥāshiyat al-Bājūrī ʿalā al-Samarqandiyyah maʿa Taqrīrāt Aḥmad ibn Aḥmad al-Ujhūrī.* N.p.: al-Maktabah al-Hāshimiyyah, n.d.

al-Majmaʿ al-Lughah al-ʿArabiyyah bi-l-Qāhirah. *al-Muʿjam al-Wasīṭ.* Edited by Ibrāhīm Muṣṭafā, Aḥmad Ḥassān al-Zayāt, and Ḥāmid ʿAbd al-Qādir. Cairo: Dār al-Daʿwah, 2008.

Mālik ibn Anas. *Muwaṭṭaʾ Mālik.* Edited by Muḥammad Muṣṭafā al-Aʿẓamī. Abu Dhabi: Muʾassasat Zāyid ibn Sulṭān Āl Nahyān li-l-Aʿmāl al-Khayriyyah wa-l-Insāniyyah, 2004.

al-Maqdisī, Ḍiyā al-Dīn Muḥammad ibn ʿAbd al-Wāḥid. *al-Aḥādīth al-Mukhtārah aw al-Mustakhraj min al-Aḥādīth al-Mukhtārah mimmā lam Yukhrijhu al-Bukhārī wa-Muslim fī Ṣaḥīḥayhimā.* 3rd ed. Edited by ʿAbd al-Malik ibn ʿAbdullāh Dahīsh. Beirut: Dār Khiḍr li-l-Ṭibāʿah wa-l-Nashr wa-l-Tawzīʿ, 2000.

al-Māwardī, Abū al-Ḥasan ʿAlī ibn Muḥammad. *Adab al-Dunyā wa-l-Dīn.* 1st ed. Jeddah: Dār al-Minhāj, 2013.

———. *al-Nukat wa-l-ʿUyūn.* Edited by al-Sayyid ʿAbd al-Maqṣūd. Beirut: Dār al-Kutub al-ʿIlmiyyah, n.d.

al-Mubārakfūrī, Ṣafī al-Raḥmaн. *Mirqāt al-Mafātīḥ Sharḥ Mishkāt al-Maṣābīḥ.* Benares, India: Jāmiʿah al-Salafiyyah, 1984.

al-Munāwī, ʿAbd al-Raʾūf Muḥammad ibn Tāj al-ʿĀrifīn. *al-Tawqīf ʿalā Muhimmāt al-Taʿārīf.* 1st ed. Edited by Jalāl al-Asyūṭī. N.p.: 2011.

al-Nakhjuwānī, Niʿmatullāh ibn Maḥmūd. *al-Fawātiḥ al-Ilāhiyyah wa-l-Mafātiḥ al-Ghaybiyyah al-Muwaḍḍiḥah li-l-Kalim al-Qurʾāniyyah wa-l-Ḥikam al-Furqāniyyah.* Beirut: Dār Kābī li-l-Nashr, 1999.

al-Nasafī, Abū al-Barakāt ʿAbdullāh. *Madārik al-Tanzīl wa-Ḥaqāʾiq al-Taʾwīl*. Edited by Yūsuf ʿAlī al-Badawī. Beirut: Dār al-Kalim al-Ṭayyib, n.d.

al-Nasāʾī, Abū ʿAbd al-Raḥmān Aḥmad ibn Shuʿayb al-Khurāsānī. *Sunan al-Nasāʾī*. Edited by ʿAbd al-Fattāḥ Abū Ghuddah. Aleppo: Maktab al-Maṭbuʿāt al-Islāmiyyah, 1986.

al-Nawawī, Abū Zakariyā Muḥyī al-Dīn Yaḥyā ibn Sharaf. *al-Minhāj Sharḥ Ṣaḥīḥ Muslim li-l-Nawawī*. Beirut: Dār Iḥyāʾ al-Turāth al-ʿArabī, 1972.

al-Naysābūrī, Abū ʿAbdullāh al-Ḥākim Muḥammad. *al-Mustadrak ʿalā al-Ṣaḥīḥayn*. Edited by Muṣṭafā ʿAbd al-Qādir ʿAṭāʾ. Beirut: Dār al-Kutub al-ʿIlmiyyah, 1990.

al-Nuʿmānī, Abū Ḥafṣ Sirāj al-Dīn ʿUmar ibn ʿAlī ibn ʿĀdil al-Ḥanbalī al-Dimashqī. *al-Lubāb fī ʿUlūm al-Kitāb*. Edited by ʿĀdil Aḥmad ʿAbd al-Mawjūd and ʿAlī Muḥammad Muʿawwaḍ. Beirut: Dār al-Kutub al-ʿIlmiyyah, 1998.

al-Qāsimī, Muḥammad Jamāl al-Dīn. *Tafsīr al-Qāsimī: al-Musammā Maḥāsin al-Taʾwīl*. Edited by Muḥammad Bāsil al-ʿUyūn. Cairo: Dār Iḥyāʾ al-Kutub al-ʿArabiyyah, 1997.

al-Qurṭubī, Abū ʿAbdullāh. *Aḥkām al-Qurʾān*. Edited by ʿAbdullāh al-Turkī. Beirut: al-Resalah Publishers, 2006.

al-Rāfiʿī, Muṣṭafā Ṣādiq. *Waḥy al-Qalam*. Edited by Muḥammad ʿAlī Kātibī. Damascus: Dār al-Qalam, 2014.

al-Rāghib al-Iṣfahānī, Abū al-Qāsim al-Ḥusayn ibn Muḥammad. *Tafṣīl al-Nashʾatayn wa-Taḥṣīl al-Saʿādatayn*. Beirut: Dār Maktabat al-Ḥayāt, 1984.

⸻. *Tafsīr al-Rāghib al-Iṣfahānī*. Edited by Muḥammad ʿAbd al-ʿAzīz al-Basyūnī. Tanta: Kulliyat al-Adāb wa-Jāmiʿat Ṭanṭā, 1999.

⸻. *al-Dharīʿah ilā Makārim al-Sharīʿah*. Edited by Abū al-Yazīd Abū Zayd al-ʿAjamī. Cairo: Dār al-Salām, 2010.

al-Rāzī, Fakhr al-Dīn Muḥammad ibn ʿUmar. *Mafātīḥ al-Ghayb aw al-Tafsīr al-Kabīr*. Beirut: Dār Iḥyāʾ al-Turāth al-ʿArabī, 1999.

al-Ṣabbān, Muḥammad ibn ʿAlī. *Ḥāshiyat Abī al-ʿIrfān Muḥammad ibn ʿAlī al-Ṣabbān ʿalā Sharḥ al-Mallawī ʿalā al-Sullam al-*

Munawraq. Edited by ʿAlawī Abū Bakr Muḥammad al-Saqqāf. Tehran: Dār al-Kutub al-Islāmiyyah, 2014.

Ṣabrī Efendi, Muṣṭafā. *Mawqif al-ʿAql wa-l-ʿIlm wa-l-ʿĀlam min Rabb al-ʿĀlamīn wa-ʿIbādat al-Mursalīn*. Beirut: Dār Iḥyāʾ al-Turāth al-ʿArabī, 1981.

al-Samarqandī, Abū al-Layth Naṣr ibn Muḥammad ibn Aḥmad. *Tanbīh al-Ghāfilīn bi-Aḥādīth al-Anbiyāʾ wa-l-Mursalīn*. 3rd ed. Edited by Yūsuf ʿAlī al-Badawī. Damascus: Dār Ibn Kathīr, 2000.

al-Shaʿrānī, ʿAbd al-Wahhāb ibn Aḥmad ibn ʿAlī. *Lawāqiḥ al-Anwār fī Ṭabaqāt al-Sādah al-Akhyār*. Cairo: Makbatat Muḥammad al-Malījī al-Kutbī wa-Akhīhi, 1897.

al-Shaʿrāwī, Muḥammad Mutawallī. *Tafsīr al-Shaʿrāwī*. [Cairo:] Dār Akhbār al-Yawm, 1991.

al-Shawkānī, Muḥammad ibn ʿAlī. *Nayl al-Awṭār*. Edited by ʿIṣām al-Dīn al-Ṣabābiṭī. Qom: Dār al-Ḥadīth, 1993.

al-Ṣiddiqī, Muḥammad ibn ʿAlī ibn Muḥammad ibn ʿIllān al-Bakrī. *Dalīl al-Fāliḥīn li-Ṭuruq Riyāḍ al-Ṣāliḥīn*. Edited by Ḍirār Shākir Yaḥyā. Damascus: Dār al-Fayḥāʾ wa-Dār al-Manhal Nāshirūn, 2018.

al-Simnānī, Rukn al-Dīn ʿAlāʾ al-Dawlah. *Tabyīn al-Maqāmāt wa-Taʿyīn al-Darajāt*. Edited by Akbar Rāshdīniyā. Translated by ʿIzzatullāh Murtaḍā. Tehran: Intishārāt-i Sukhan, 2017.

al-Suhaylī, Abū al-Qāsim ʿAbd al-Raḥman ibn ʿAbdullāh ibn Aḥmad. *al-Rawḍ al-Anaf wa-l-Mashraʿ al-Rawī fī Mā Ishtamala ʿalayhi Ḥadīth al-Sīrah wa-Iḥtawā*. Edited by ʿUmar ʿAbd al-Salām. Beirut: Dār Iḥyāʾ al-Turāth al-ʿArabī, 2000.

al-Ṭabarānī, Abū al-Qāsim Sulaymān ibn Aḥmad. *al-Muʿjam al-Ṣaghīr*. Edited by Muḥammad Shakūr Amrīr. Beirut: al-Maktab al-Islāmī wa-Dār ʿImār, 1985.

———. *al-Muʿjam al-Kabīr*. Edited by Ḥamdī ʿAbd al-Majīd. Cairo: Maktabat Ibn Taymiyyah, n.d.

al-Tirmidhī, Muḥammad ibn ʿĪsā. *al-Jāmiʿ al-Ṣaḥīḥ: wa-Huwa Sunan al-Tirmidhī*. Edited by Aḥmad Shākir. Cairo: Muṣṭafā al-Bābī al-Ḥalabī, 1976.

al-Wāḥidī, Abū al-Ḥasan ʿAlī ibn Aḥmad. *al-Wasīṭ fī Tafsīr al-Qurʾān al-Majīd*. Edited by ʿĀdil ʿAbd al-Mawjūd. Beirut: Dār al-Kutub al-ʿIlmiyyah, n.d.

al-Yūsī, al-Ḥasan ibn Masʿūd. *Rasāʾil Abī ʿAlī al-Ḥasan ibn Masʿūd al-Yūsī*. Edited by Fāṭimah Khalīl al-Qiblī. Cairo: Dār al-Thaqāfah, 1981.

al-Zabīdī, al-Sayyid Muḥammad Murtaḍā. *Tāj al-ʿArūs min Jawāhir al-Qāmūs*. Kuwait: Wizārat al-Irshād wa-l-Anbā, 1965.

al-Zamakhsharī, Maḥmūd ibn ʿUmar. *al-Kashshāf ʿan Ghawāmiḍ al-Tanzīl wa-ʿUyūn al-Aqāwīl*. Edited by ʿĀdil ʿAbd al-Mawjūd. Riyadh: Maktabat al-ʿUbaykān, 1998.

www.ingramcontent.com/pod-product-compliance
Lightning Source LLC
Chambersburg PA
CBHW060503160726
47992CB00003B/1307